P9-DZY-305

She Touched the World

She Touched the World

Laura Bridgman, Deaf-Blind Pioneer

by Sally Hobart Alexander
and Robert Alexander

CLARION BOOKS ❖ NEW YORK

To all those who live gracefully with disability,
and to our beloved friend Nancy Markham Alberts,
who lived with grace

Clarion Books
a Houghton Mifflin Company imprint
215 Park Avenue South, New York, NY 10003
Copyright © 2008 by Sally Hobart Alexander and Robert Alexander

The text was set in 12-point Schneidler.

www.clarionbooks.com

Printed in the U.S.A.

Library of Congress Cataloging-in-Publication Data
Alexander, Sally Hobart.
She touched the world : Laura Bridgman, deaf-blind pioneer / by Sally Hobart Alexander and Robert Alexander.
p. cm.
Includes bibliographical references.
ISBN 978-0-618-85299-4
1. Bridgman, Laura Dewey, 1829–1889—Juvenile literature. 2. Deaf-blind women—
United States—Biography—Juvenile literature. I. Alexander, Robert Joseph, 1944– II. Title.
HV1624.B7A44 2008
362.4'1092—dc22
[B]
2007034978

VB 10 9 8 7 6 5 4 3 2

Contents

Acknowledgments   vii

Important People in Laura Bridgman's Life   ix

Introduction   xi

1   A Delicate Plant   1

2   In Touch   6

3   Friend and Frustrations   12

4   "A Very Unusually Tall [Man]"   16

5   Taken Away   23

6   What Can Laura Do?   26

7   Words! Words! Words!   32

8   Schoolgirl   38

9   Windows Open   44

10   Weapon or Masterpiece?   50

11   "Is God Ever Surprised?"   56

12   Famous   61

13   Farewells   68

Afterword   76

Source Notes   85

Bibliography   94

Websites   96

Index   97

Acknowledgments

This story would never have come to life without the remarkable generosity of three individuals, and we give them our inadequate thanks: Joan Friedberg, cofounder of Pittsburgh's Beginning with Books, for planting the idea; Jan Seymour-Ford, Perkins research librarian, for tireless hunting and gathering; and Cynthia Ingraham, east-central regional representative of the Helen Keller National Center for Deaf-Blind Youths and Adults, for extraordinary expertise and the willingness to share it.

Other individuals and institutions provided critical help, and we can't thank them enough: the Perkins School for the Blind, Watertown, Massachusetts; the Library of Congress; Point Park University, Pittsburgh; Sally's beloved Tuesday morning writing group; Kendra Marcus, Book Stop Literary Agency; our editor, Lynne Polvino, and Dinah Stevenson, publisher of Clarion Books; June Tulikangas, former Perkins librarian; Bruce Blakeslee, photographer, Perkins School for the Blind; Spiro Pipakis, director of the Access Technology Center, Blindness and Rehabilitation Services of Pittsburgh; Dr. Sharna Olfman, professor of psychology, Point Park University; Dr. Catherine Palmer, professor of audiology, Eye and Ear Institute, Pittsburgh; Dr. Jonathon Erlen, professor of history, University of Pittsburgh; Joe McNulty, director, Helen Keller National Center for Deaf-Blind Youths and Adults; Leslie Alexander; Dr. James Greenberg, pediatric anesthesiologist, University of Pittsburgh Medical Center; Debbie Holzapfel, educational assistant, Pennsylvania Training and

Technical Assistance Network; the Overbrook School for the Blind; the Pennsylvania Deaf-Blind Project; Jackie Brennan; Dr. Terence Starz, arthritis and internal medicine, University of Pittsburgh Medical Center; Anna Mihalega, Point Park University reference librarian; Kathy Ayres; Karen Lynn Williams; Christopher LaGarde; Ilse Heymann; Ellen Miller; Marilyn Oettinger; Marti Wallen; Lynn Vuocolo; and Dr. Ron Linden, professor of political science, University of Pittsburgh.

And readers: Miriam Kalnicki, Jason Feldstein, Jessica Kurs-Lasky, and Lisa Ochs.

And consultants: Kate, Claire, and Madeline Zimmerman; Jake and Luke Carra; Taylor and Garrett Wallen; Zetta Murphy; Ken Wotjczak; Barbara Krieger, Rauner Library, Dartmouth College; and Martha Berg.

Important People in Laura Bridgman's Life

Laura's Family

Daniel Bridgman
Laura's father
December 12, 1800 – November 28, 1868

Harmony Downer Bridgman
Laura's mother
February 27, 1804 – April 16, 1891

Mary
sister
August 20, 1825 – February 7, 1832

Collina
sister
August 26, 1827 – February 5, 1832

Laura
December 21, 1829 – May 24, 1889

Addison Daniel
brother
August 10, 1832 – November 16, 1916

John Downer
brother
July 9, 1834 – June 21, 1919

Milo
brother
November 2, 1838 – April 2, 1839

Mary
sister
January 25, 1842 – November 14, 1859

Frances Collina
sister
February 18, 1845 – ?

Ellen "Nellie" Diantha
sister
April 29, 1850 – April 20, 1904

Laura's Close Friends and Teachers

Asa Tenney

Dr. Samuel Gridley Howe

Lydia Drew   Mary Swift   Sarah Wight

Oliver Caswell

Laura Bridgman, early 1840s. (Perkins School for the Blind)

Introduction

If you had lived in 1841, the name Laura Bridgman would have echoed through your home, your school, your neighborhood. It would have rung out in the streets of Boston, in the halls of Congress, and across the ocean to England and Europe and beyond. By the time Laura Bridgman was twelve years old, she was that famous.

Like all children, you would have loved and admired her. You would have named your favorite doll after her. . . . And then you would have poked out the doll's eyes.

1

A Delicate Plant

On December 21, 1829, in Etna, a town very near Hanover, New Hampshire, Harmony Bridgman gave birth to her third child, a "delicate plant" of a girl named Laura. Her eyes were blue as cornflowers and seemed to take in everything. But her legs and arms jerked from what doctors called "fits," making her very weak.

Her parents raised animals on their farm and knew about sickly newborns. They worried that any one of these fits could damage their daughter, or even kill her.

But Harmony and Daniel Bridgman may have been hesitant to call on a doctor to treat Laura. Trained physicians in the early 1800s still believed that the body was made up of four elements called "humors": blood, phlegm, black bile, and choler, or yellow bile. If these humors were out of balance, a person grew ill.

For most ailments, doctors used one of five approaches to restore balance to the humors: bleeding, blistering, cleansing, medicating, or sweating. They always tried sweating first, hoping to allow the body to get rid of the bad or excess humors naturally. Healers might try hot

An advertisement for a nineteenth-century medicine that claims to cure "all disorders of the Blood . . . and all other Humors." (Library of Congress)

baths, heavy blankets, or steam rooms to make their patients sweat. If this technique didn't work, doctors used harsher cures, such as bleeding—cutting a vein and drawing large quantities of blood from the person. They also used leeches, blood-sucking invertebrates that were attached to the patient's skin near a vein.

In addition, doctors sometimes placed burning-hot compresses wherever the sickness seemed to be located. These compresses gave people second-degree burns that blistered. From the blisters came a liquid that doctors thought was bad humors. In reality, however, the burns often caused infection and made the patients even sicker.

If that wasn't bad enough, physicians often gave ipecac or other drugs to make their patients vomit or go to the bathroom, believing this would purge the body of the unwanted humors. Calomel was a favorite medicine of the time; it was given in large doses to cleanse the body. What physicians didn't know then was that calomel slowly poisoned its users. Other drugs, such as camphor and opium, were also administered to help patients sleep.

At the time of Laura's fits, only about 10 percent of the population ever sought medical help. One reason for this was that a doctor required payment, and few people had the necessary funds. But the main reason was distrust. Over and over again, people saw that doctors made their patients worse, not better.

There is no evidence that Harmony and Daniel sought medical treatment for Laura's fits. But since they did employ a physician a few years later when Laura and her sisters became ill, it is likely the Bridgmans had a doctor's help with her fits, too.

When Laura was twenty months old, the fits disappeared. She began to walk and explore her surroundings, chasing after her older sisters, Mary and Collina, with the quickness of a bunny. She darted from the loom to the spinning wheel, eager to see, hear, and touch everything. Laura even experimented with words, and could put short sentences together by the time she was two years old. Her parents concluded that she was their brightest child.

But a few months later, in February 1832, Laura and her sisters were stricken with what doctors said was scarlet fever. The disease, which caused a rash and facial flush, was common at the time.

Years later Laura recalled, "I was saturated with very bad sores on my chin and neck and on my lowest right leg and other parts of the body. . . . My dearest mother was so painfully apprehensive that there was great danger of my dying."

Laura lived in this farmhouse in Etna, New Hampshire, until October 1837. (Perkins School for the Blind, photo by Janice Seymour-Ford)

And understandably so. Many children did die of the disease. In the 1850s scarlet fever (often called "the plague among children") reached epidemic proportions. Doctors knew neither its cause nor its cure.

In a dark bedroom, Laura lay near Collina and Mary, all three drooping like flowers in dry soil. Their fevers raged.

Laura wasn't aware of four-year-old Collina's death on February 5, 1832, or of Mary's, at the age of six, on February 7. Through the fog of her illness, she knew only the darkness of the room and her mother's hand giving her medicine—no doubt, calomel.

Yet Laura lived on. Her fever burned for five more weeks, destroying her sight. The infection spread, consuming her hearing and almost all of her senses of smell and taste.

After her fever finally passed, Laura remained sick for another five months, suffering from chronic pain in both eyes. Occasionally, she repeated the word "dark," perhaps in an attempt to describe her new blindness. Harmony gave birth to another child, a boy named Addison, but Laura was too ill to be aware of any change in the farmhouse.

Slowly, Laura recovered. A year passed before she could walk short distances because her feet were inflamed. Her family wrapped them with poultices—heated cloths filled with moist, soft bread, meal, or clay—to soothe and heal them. Still another year elapsed before she could sit up all day without support. A new baby, John, arrived, and Addison toddled underfoot.

Finally, when she was about five, Laura became strong and healthy again. Like any child, she wanted to explore. But how could she? She was completely deaf and blind. Her world was silent, and gray as an overcast sky. Her once vast vocabulary had disappeared from her memory. The last word Harmony heard her speak was "book."

Harmony and Daniel continued to worry about their daughter and wondered how she could survive. At this point, Addison was talking, and John could say a few words. Every day they increased their vocabularies and learned more about the world around them.

But in Laura's world without sound, there were no words. There wasn't even the concept of language. She couldn't communicate and grow the way her brothers did. Without sight, she couldn't learn from gestures or facial expressions.

At five, she was the oldest child, yet she was far behind her brothers in her development. Her parents considered her imprisoned in her own body and feared that her chances of leading a full life had been lost along with her hearing and sight.

But Laura had hands and feet, ten fingers and ten toes. She still had touch, and something more—an endless curiosity.

2

In Touch

Laura touched everything in the farmhouse and could tell one object from another by its texture, temperature, size, and weight. The beds, chairs, tables, and dishes attached to her memory as separate feelings and distinct items. She didn't have a name for these objects, but she knew them.

She also knew her parents, Harmony and Daniel: large forms like furniture—except for their movement, the touch of their hands, their warmth and soft surfaces. Two smaller forms, Addison and John, were like little furless dogs, always underfoot, always squirming out of reach.

Once Laura had familiarized herself with the contents of the farmhouse, she ventured outside. Dewy grass, feathery flowers, jagged rocks and smooth ones, rough pole-like trees, small tender berries, prickly bushes—Laura explored them all by touch. She tugged on the thick matted wool of the sheep; she felt the soft muzzle of a calf and giggled when he sucked her fingers.

Laura's entire world was near, close by. The sun was heat on her face,

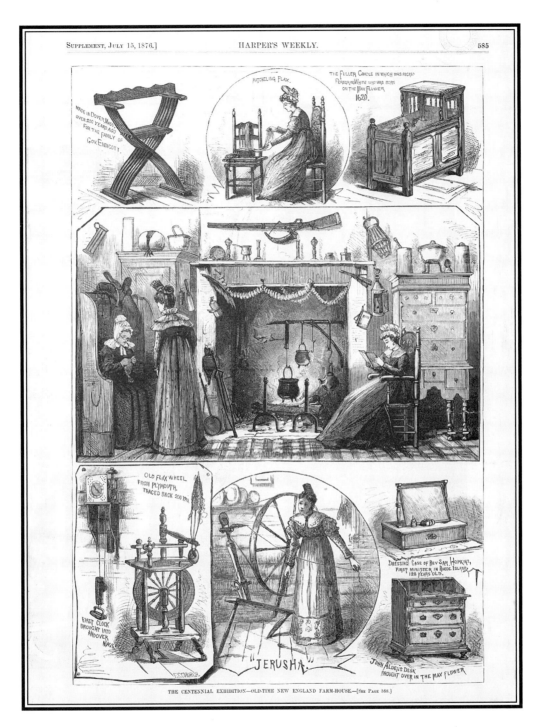

These illustrations show interior scenes of a typical mid-nineteenth-century New England farmhouse, including a spinning wheel at the bottom center. (Library of Congress)

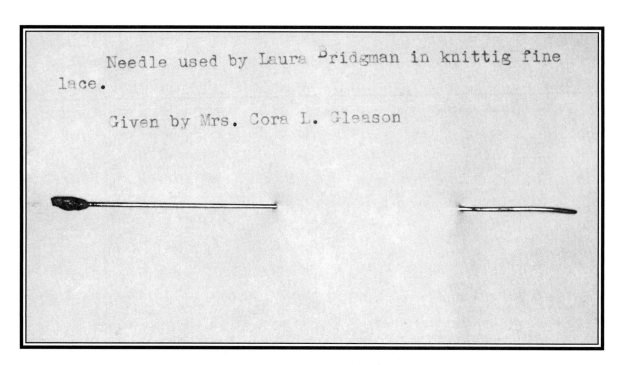

Needle used by Laura Bridgman in knittig fine lace.

Given by Mrs. Cora L. Gleason

This is a needle that Laura used. (Perkins School for the Blind, photo by Bruce Blakeslee)

not a distant ball in the sky. Mountains were sloped, uneven paths to climb, not faraway peaks that touched the horizon.

Day by day, Laura clung to Harmony's skirt or clutched her hand, reaching out to follow her movements, imitating everything she did. Soon she could knit, braid, iron, churn butter, set the table, and bake little tarts. She learned to sew, finding the needle's eye with the tip of her tongue, which is even more sensitive than fingertips. While most people learn these skills by watching, Laura learned by feeling. It was as if her hands and fingers could see.

But often Laura's hands were idle; she had nothing to do.

As a farmer's wife, Harmony had to work constantly. Not only did she feed and care for Laura and her brothers, but she also did all the house-work, sewed all the clothes, made soap and candles, and tended the sheep,

Eventually, Laura learned to knit intricate lace. (Perkins School for the Blind, photo by Bruce Blakeslee)

Samples of Laura's handiwork, including beaded tatting for a lady's collar. In the 1800s it was fashionable to wear detachable collars like this one. (Perkins School for the Blind, photo by Bruce Blakeslee)

bees, and chickens. Daniel ran the farm and served two sessions in the New Hampshire legislature. He also helped to run the Hanover town government.

They were often too busy to tend to Laura, so she spent much of her time alone, sitting, rocking, crossing and uncrossing her legs. She felt the chair's smooth wood, the fierce heat from the fireplace. *Rock, rock, rock.* Minutes, hours passed slowly. Time was her enemy.

In addition to being busy, the Bridgmans were formal people. They rarely hugged Laura or her brothers. Perhaps they were prim and proper, like the stereotype of old-fashioned New Englanders. Or maybe the deaths of Mary and Collina had made them wary of feeling too great an attachment to their children.

As a creature of touch, Laura probably yearned for more physical affection from her parents. But Laura wasn't like any child the Bridgmans had ever experienced. They loved and cared for her, but they didn't always know what to do with her. For instance, they didn't think to give her a doll. So Laura turned an old boot into a plaything. She filled it with her treasures: stones, feathers, and wool from the sheared sheep.

"I had a man's large boot, which I called my little baby," she later recalled. "I enjoyed myself in playing with the articifical [sic] baby very much. I never knew how to kiss my boot or any of my folks. . . . I did not feel so solitary with a baby as I should have felt if I had not had one."

3

Friend and Frustrations

One important person in Laura's life was an old bachelor and handyman, Asa Tenney. Uncle Asa, as Laura later called him, did odd jobs for the Bridgmans and some of their neighbors in Hanover.

"Mr. Tenney was one of my greatest and best benefactors," Laura remembered. "He loved me as if I was his own daughter. . . . I felt much farther familiar with him than my father."

Although Asa Tenney was not formally educated, he became Laura's first teacher. He guided her around the farm for hours at a time, introducing her to the flowers and to the brook at the bottom of the hill. He carried her to meet her neighbors. He helped her search for berries, nuts, apples, and eggs. He placed birds' nests in her hands and let her hold the babies inside. To Laura, birds were not flying beasts that soared to the clouds but fragile creatures with beating chests to be held tenderly.

"My dearest friend, Mr. Tenney, gave me a thin tin plate with the edge printed in the blind alphabet," she recalled. "I occupied it daily with much pleasure."

At the time Laura received this gift, she had no idea what the raised

The tin plate Mr. Tenney gave Laura was similar to this nineteenth-century ABC plate. Made of ceramic or tin, with the alphabet raised up along the surface of the rim, such plates were popular gifts for children in the 1800s. (Courtesy of Ruby Lane Childhood Antiques, Springfield, Mass., photo by Jim Greenberg)

print letters were. She simply enjoyed the experience of touching the unusual markings that distinguished her plate from others used by her family.

With Asa and her parents, Laura invented basic ways of communicating:

- ◆ Pushing meant go.
- ◆ Pulling meant come.
- ◆ Patting on the head meant good.
- ◆ Patting on the back or stamping the floor meant bad.
- ◆ Hand to lips, as if tipping a cup, meant drink.

But for a girl as curious and bright as Laura, these gestures weren't enough. Over and over again she tried to make herself understood . . . and failed. Over and over again her parents and Asa tried to think of a way to teach her basic facts . . . and failed. There was so much Laura didn't know. For instance, she understood that the fireplace provided heat to keep her warm during cold weather, but she didn't realize that it could burn.

Once she dropped her cat, Blackie, onto the blazing logs of the fireplace. Suddenly, footsteps rushed, feet stamped. Hands shoved. Everywhere vibrations stirred, whirred.

Laura knew something bad had happened—she sensed that she'd done something wrong. But what? Her mother had no way of explaining it to her. What signs could she use to communicate that fire had burned Blackie's skin and fur, and that it was probably going to kill the beloved cat? Blackie managed to get out of the farmhouse and never returned, so Harmony couldn't put Laura's hand on the cat's injuries, then move her hand toward the fire to make the cause-and-effect connection. She couldn't let Laura feel how limp and lifeless the cat would have been after the accident.

Although this incident was the most dramatic example of the gaps in Laura's knowledge, nearly every day she attempted something dangerous or exasperating. Harmony's hands constantly saved her from a fall, a burn, a cut. Laura grew increasingly frustrated.

During one of her outings with Asa, Laura searched each of his pockets for a bottle of milk. For several weeks she'd been feeding an orphaned lamb, and she wanted to feed it again. Asa didn't have the bottle. The lamb had grown old enough to graze and feed itself, but Asa couldn't explain this to Laura. She became more and more upset until finally she pulled off Asa's glasses and crushed them. He didn't have the heart to punish her.

A few days later, as Harmony applied oil to Laura's eyelids, perhaps to soothe the stinging pain she continued to feel in her eyes, Laura suddenly grabbed the jar and hurled it across the room, smashing it. Harmony's foot stamped, sending angry vibrations throughout the farmhouse.

As she grew older, Laura received fewer pats on the head, even fewer embraces. Every day she grew more confused, felt more unable to get what she wanted. Several times a week her anger rose until, like lava, it erupted.

Charles Dickens (1812–70) was one of the most popular novelists of the nineteenth century. Some of his most famous works are A Christmas Carol, Great Expectations, David Copperfield, *and* The Old Curiosity Shop, *a novel that was produced in raised print so that it could be read by the blind. Dickens wrote about injustice; he wanted to better conditions for the poor and helpless. It is no wonder, then, that he was so fascinated by Laura. (Library of Congress)*

She struck her mother. Daniel stamped his foot and grabbed Laura to restrain her. But increasingly, Laura lashed out. Gloom spread through the household.

As the famous English novelist Charles Dickens later wrote about Laura: "Those who cannot be 'taught' by reason can only be controlled by force; and this . . . must soon have reduced her to a worse condition than that of the beasts . . . , but for timely and un-hoped-for aid."

Fortunately, that aid was near.

4

"A Very Unusually Tall [Man]"

Every May, Daniel Bridgman and the other selectmen of Hanover had to work on the town's tax bills. As farmers, they were extremely busy in the spring, so they decided to hire a Dartmouth College student named James Barrett to prepare these accounts.

When James arrived at the Bridgman farm to begin working on the bills, he spied seven-year-old Laura and became fascinated. Between tasks he sat with her, giving her his pocket watch and other objects. Laura explored the items with deep concentration and, when possible, opened, closed, and took them apart. James immediately saw the spark of her remarkable intellect. In 1837 he spoke to one of his professors, Dr. Reuben Mussey, and invited him to observe Laura himself.

Mussey agreed with James that Laura was not only desperate to learn but also teachable. This was an extraordinary conclusion. In the early 1800s people who were "just" deaf or "just" blind were considered impossible to educate. Somebody like Laura, who was doubly disabled, was considered absolutely hopeless.

16

This lithograph shows the Dartmouth College campus in the mid-1830s, around the time James Barrett was a student there. (Library of Congress)

Mussey placed a letter in a local newspaper describing Laura. It read, in part:

> Her name is Laura D. Bridgman, seven years old, a girl of middling stature for her age and of a pretty uniform health. When about two years old she lost her hearing altogether and all distinctness of vision by scarlet fever. She has never [since] given evidence of hearing any sort of sound, but she can perceive light enough to enable her to tell where the windows are during the day, and is attracted by a lighted taper at evening. A white cloth or sheet of white paper placed near to her right eye so as to reflect a strong light, engages her attention; so does the hand, waved from side to side between her eye and the window. The left eye is wholly destroyed.

The letter was seen by Dr. Samuel Gridley Howe, the head of the New England Institution for the Education of the Blind, the first school for blind children in America.

Both a doctor and an educator, Samuel Gridley Howe was an exceptional man. After graduating from Harvard Medical School in 1824, he chose not to open a medical office. Instead, using his own funds, he traveled to Greece and fought alongside the Greeks in their war for independence against the Turks. For six years he shared their encampments, their food, and their risks, and ministered to the wounded and dying.

Around the time Laura was born, Howe returned to America to raise money to continue to help the Greeks after the war. And raise money he did—sixty thousand dollars, a huge sum then, equal to more than a million dollars today. He used it to feed people who were starving, and he also gathered clothing and other supplies, which he distributed back in Greece.

Soon afterward, his friend John Fisher asked Howe to become the head of the very first American school for the blind. The New England Institution for the Education of the Blind, chartered in 1829, had been waiting for the right director. Fisher had visited institutions for blind children in Europe and hoped Howe would model the American school on them.

Howe set off to study those centers in Paris and Berlin. While in Europe, however, he couldn't resist getting involved in another war of independence, this time the Polish struggle against Russia. After visiting the Berlin School for the Blind, Howe was arrested and thrown into a dungeon. The authorities claimed he'd transported money and supplies for the Poles. Since Howe's involvement wasn't supported by the American government, his hopes of regaining his freedom were slim. Fortunately, however, an American friend grew suspicious when Howe failed to show up for an appointment. The friend began a search, which led to his rescue.

Finally, in July 1832 Howe settled down to the business of opening and

A portrait of Samuel Gridley Howe (1801–76) as a young man. (Perkins School for the Blind)

running a school, admitting two blind students, who studied at his father's house in Boston and later at the home of Thomas H. Perkins on Pearl Street.

During his first five years as director of the Institution, Howe grew interested in educating all kinds of handicapped people. Early in 1837 he traveled to Hartford, Connecticut, to meet a thirty-year-old woman named Julia Brace who, like Laura, was both deaf and blind. At the time, there were 250 known Deaf-Blind mutes in the country, but none were educated. Despite his efforts, Howe could not teach Julia the manual alphabet, the twenty-six different finger positions first published in a book by Juan Pablo Bonet in 1620. Julia just didn't seem interested.

When Howe heard of a new Deaf-Blind girl in Hanover, New Hampshire, he lost no time in traveling there, taking advantage of a trip he had already planned with the poet Henry Wadsworth Longfellow and other friends.

One day in July 1837 Laura sensed unusual vibrations in the air. All morning her mother's hands had felt edgy, anxious. Laura perceived trouble, and her heart fluttered.

Asa paced inside the farmhouse. When Laura reached to touch him, his arms felt rigid, and his hands were balled into fists. Abruptly, he left. What was wrong?

Then hot July air blew in through the open doorway. The farmhouse jumped with unfamiliar footsteps. Laura's feet caught the nervousness, felt everything. Her feet heard. Suddenly, a hand took hers.

"I shrunk myself as hastily as I had strength. . . . He seemed to be [such] a very unusually tall [man] . . . that it made me much repelled," she later recalled.

Howe found Laura to be fiery and spirited—and altogether wonderful. He noted she had a well-formed figure, a strongly marked, nervous temperament, and "a large and beautifully-shaped head."

Howe was delighted about Laura's head because he believed in phrenology. Phrenologists thought each section of the brain had an external aspect, a raised part on the skull. The larger the bump, the greater the ability. To Howe, each bump on Laura's head indicated secret power, promise.

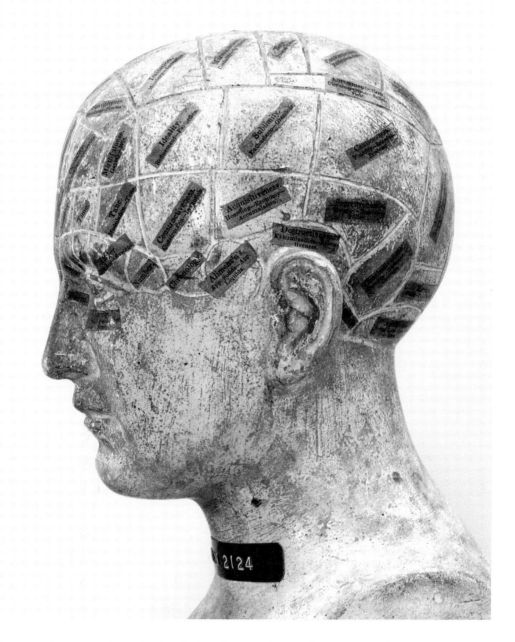

This somewhat grimy plaster head with identifying words pasted on it was used to teach phrenology. According to biographer Ernest Freeberg, Howe's school had a collection of hundreds of skulls. "As the most enthusiastic officer of the Boston Phrenological Society," writes Freeberg, "Howe became the caretaker of the group's extensive collection—a scientific gallery of skulls, busts, and plaster casts of famous heads." Howe kept many of these skulls in his office. (Perkins School for the Blind, photo by Bruce Blakeslee)

Next, Howe offered Laura a small silver pencil case. She snatched the present and threw it across the room.

Despite Laura's poor manners, Howe wanted her to come to Boston—to the Institution—to live with him and his sister Jeannette in their apartment. He was sure he could reach her, teach her. She had a bumpy skull, a lively personality, and hands that were like antennae. He believed he could become "the father of her mind."

5

Taken Away

On October 12, 1837, Laura discovered her mother packing her belongings, even her boot. What did this mean? Laura paced from the chest of drawers to the travel case. Tension surged through her arms and legs, tightening her muscles, making her cheek twitch.

Outside, Asa stood by the carriage. As he hugged her, Laura felt him shudder. His arm around her shoulder sagged. Something was very wrong, and Laura began to tremble. She didn't know then that Asa didn't think the school would do her any good. He thought *he* could care for her best.

Her parents helped her into the carriage, and she felt the wheels begin to turn. But Addison and John weren't with them. Where were they going?

A frosty wind nipped her face as the carriage bounced along. There was no sun to warm her skin or dry her tears. Laura knew something unusual was going on, and the change frightened her. Sitting between her parents, she felt little comfort. In her world of clouds and silence, she couldn't understand what was happening.

Later she recalled, "My parents conducted me to the Institute in Pearl

Street. . . . I dreaded leaving home so much that it made me shed an abundance of tears. . . . The time elapsed so very heavily and painfully."

When they reached the city of Boston, after traveling about three or four days, vibrations of other carriages, of horses' hooves, of people's shouts all bombarded her. Laura must have been relieved to enter the calm of the Institution, unfamiliar as it was. Still, her insides ached, and she fumed with vexation. "I kept clinging on my dear parents so as not to let them escape from me, but did not succeed in detaining them. . . . At the very moment that I lost them, I burst into the bitterest of tears. Miss J. Howe, one of Doctor's sisters, . . . tried to pacify and soothe me, but my

This daguerreotype (an early type of photograph) shows a mid-nineteenth-century horse-drawn carriage. The Bridgmans probably took Laura to Boston in a carriage much like this one. (Library of Congress)

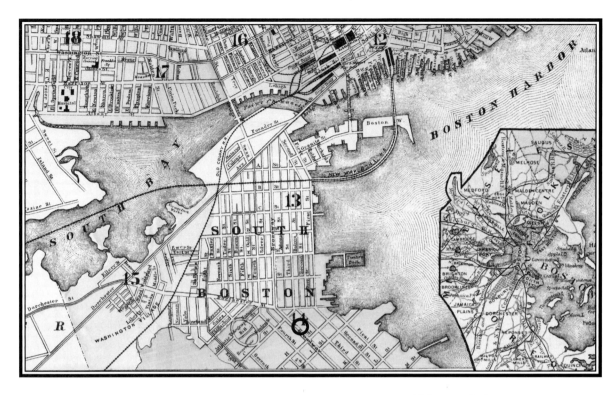

This map of South Boston in 1881 shows many of the same streets Laura would have walked. At the bottom is a black circle indicating the location of the Institution. (Collection of Fred and Ruth Alexander)

poor heart was too full of sorrow and trouble. I was so much more home-sick to retrace my steps . . . than I could bear."

A month later, on November 8, 1837, Samuel Gridley Howe described a much easier adjustment for Laura in a letter to her parents. "Your little girl is in very good health and spirits. She was rather dull for two days after you left her, and cried two or three times, but after that, she became very lively, and I do not think that she repines at all for her home now."

Laura probably cried more than two or three times, but eventually her eager spirit took over. Her curiosity ignited, blazed. Her hands went to work, touching, exploring everything in Jeannette's and Doctor's apartment. Before long, she could move from room to room freely. Soon this new world would become manageable, familiar, her own.

6

What Can Laura Do?

As soon as Laura seemed calm in her new surroundings, Howe set to work. First, he administered a series of mild electric shocks, hoping to restart some of her missing senses. He pressed "one piece of metal against the mucous membrane of the nose, and another against the tongue" and thought he'd affected "the nerves of taste." Laura said, in fact, it was "like medicine."

This technique was not a common practice in the 1830s. In earlier centuries, however, electricity had been used in attempts to restore sight to the blind. In fact, as far back as the Roman Empire, shocks from electric fish were used to cure a range of ailments, including persistent headaches and epilepsy. According to some accounts, one of the Emperor Nero's freed slaves stepped on an electric ray while walking on the beach. Although he suffered severe pain from the sting, the discomfort he'd been enduring in that foot, probably from gout, mysteriously disappeared. After that, a respected physician of the time used electric fish to treat painful disorders and claimed that it gave his patients relief.

In giving shocks to Laura, Howe most likely was following the practice

Samuel Gridley Howe moved the New England Institution for the Education of the Blind from his father's home to this Pearl Street location in 1833, and it stayed there until 1839, when it moved to South Boston and became known as the Perkins Institution. (Perkins School for the Blind)

Benjamin Franklin (1706–90) was one of the most famous of the Founding Fathers of the United States, as well as an important author, printer, politician, diplomat, philosopher, scientist, and inventor. He was also a practicing physician. Most people know that his experiments with electricity (including flying a kite in a storm) led to several important discoveries and inventions. But few realize that he put his knowledge of electricity to use on his patients. This print shows him looking at an electrical device to his right, while lightning strikes a building outside the window to his left. (Library of Congress)

of the famous American statesman Benjamin Franklin, who had also worked as a doctor. He had applied "electrotherapy" with some success to treat psychological problems such as depression. Franklin also tried this treatment on paralyzed patients, although he was not able to get their limbs to work again.

When the electric shocks failed to produce any change in Laura, Howe examined and prodded and studied her. He drew the following conclusions about how she experienced the world:

Sight: Until the age of seven, Laura could see light with her right eye, from a candle or through a window, and maybe even some colors and shapes. Unfortunately, sometime before she met Howe, she bumped that eye into a spindle and became totally blind. Still, she understood the difference between light and dark.

Sound: To Laura, the vibrations from people's footsteps or voices were sound. She "heard" with her feet. "Sound comes up through the floor to my feet, and up to my head," she explained. She once told her teacher "something in my right foot hears." When asked about her left foot, she replied, "I cannot hear good with my left." Amazingly, she could tell one person's vibrations from those of another.

Taste: Laura could tell the difference between meat and vegetables, but probably more from the texture than from the taste. She was best at detecting acidic flavors, such as vinegar. Throughout her life she didn't care as much about eating as most people. When she was upset, she often stopped eating altogether and just drank black coffee—once for two whole weeks.

Smell: Laura never brought any objects to her nose. She could smell only very strong fragrances, such as onions and ammonia. The sense never seemed to be of any importance to her.

Touch: This sense was so developed that Laura could feel lint or dirt on her clothing. She recognized anyone she'd met by the slightest touch of a hand, no matter how long it had been since the encounter with the person—once as long as six years. Laura always surprised people by identifying her friends by a brief touch of their hands or clothes. She could tell if Howe wore a new coat, even if it was of the same material and style as the old one. She also could tell people's moods by the feel of their footsteps, by touching their faces, by the way they took her hand. If they grabbed it in haste, for instance, she could sense displeasure.

Pain: Laura cried only from sadness. When she felt pain from an injury, she tried to get rid of it by jumping and doing muscular exercise.

Noise: Laura had a "good, hearty laugh." She was noisy at play and occasionally made other noises Howe called "disagreeable and unladylike." He decided right away to stop them, worried that they would keep her from being accepted by other people. Still, for the rest of her life Laura persisted in making them. G. Stanley Hall, a psychologist who studied her, said she wouldn't have been aware of the sounds unless she touched her throat and felt the vibrations of her vocal cords. Yet her teachers complained often of Laura's "refusal to grow still and gentle." They thought she made the noises on purpose. After Laura learned to communicate, she seemed to confirm their suspicions, bragging that "God gave me much voice."

Eventually, Howe tried to compromise with her. If she was quiet in public, he would give her permission to step into a closet, close the door, and make as many sounds as she wanted.

Speech: Laura could say the words "doctor," "ship," and "pie," and spoke these words as often as possible. With great effort, she also learned to say the word "baby." During her years at the Institution she developed at least fifty different sounds for the people she knew. All these names were repeated one-syllable sounds, such as "Fi-Fi." If one of her teachers married and took her spouse's name, Laura changed the sound for that person.

Today, experts think Laura could have been taught to speak. But Howe tried teaching her, didn't succeed, and gave up. He didn't like the masculine sound of her voice and thought people would shun her.

At the end of Howe's examinations, he concluded that Laura's long illness had erased almost all memories of sight and sound and smell and

English philosopher John Locke (1632–1704) coined the term "tabula rasa." He didn't believe that ideas were part of the mind at birth. Babies came into the world, he said, with minds that were like blank slates. Ideas entered the mind through experiences of seeing, hearing, touching, smelling, and tasting. Howe, on the other hand, followed thinkers of his day who argued that people were born with abilities, or "faculties," such as the ability to learn language. Among these faculties, according to Howe and others, was a desire to do good and help others. (Library of Congress)

taste. Yet that didn't mean that her mind was a blank slate, a *tabula rasa,* empty of all images, as some philosophers thought. Howe debated with people around New England about what ideas came at birth and what ideas were learned. Laura provided a "living laboratory" to test these theories.

He concluded that Laura's mind was a "soul jailed to a body," active, struggling to communicate with the world outside and the world within herself. He resolved to free her from that prison.

7

Words! Words! Words!

Of course, Laura didn't know Doctor's thoughts. She didn't know he was debating between two different approaches to working with her:

- ♦ Give her random signs based on the signs she had already invented with her parents and Asa
- ♦ Teach her the alphabet so that she could express anything she wanted

Howe wrote that teaching her letters seemed very difficult, yet he decided to try that approach.

Laura was not aware of Dr. Howe's goal as she sat with him and another person, his assistant, Lydia Drew. On the table in front of her were everyday objects: a knife, a spoon, a book, and a key. Laura touched them all, recognizing them, though not able to identify them by name.

She picked up the key. It felt very much like the key she had used at home to lock her boot in the cupboard. But wait! This key had a piece of paper fastened to it, paper with several letters of the alphabet embossed—raised—so that Laura could feel their shape with her fingertip. (Another "touch reading" system had already been invented by the young blind Frenchman Louis Braille, which used a series of six raised dots instead of letters, but Laura didn't learn it. The Braille system wasn't widely employed until well past the time of Laura's schooling.)

Now, sitting between Doctor and Miss Drew, Laura ran her finger over the raised letters. She felt the other objects and found that they also had raised-print labels attached to them. Laura ran her finger over each object and over each label. As her hands

Here is Nathaniel Hawthorne's The Scarlet Letter *with the title in both the raised-print alphabet and Braille.* (Perkins School for the Blind, *photo by Bruce Blakeslee*)

worked, her mind stirred. The knife and spoon were different from each other. The lines of the raised word "knife" were different from the raised lines for "spoon."

Stroke. Tap. Scratch gently with a fingernail. Laura concentrated. The different combinations of raised letters *belonged* to each object. Eventually, the words pushed into her mind, her consciousness. She began to understand that the embossed labels *identified* the objects.

Doctor patted her head. Miss Drew hugged her.

Laura smiled. She moved closer to the table, her mind racing. Her heart, too.

Next, Howe removed the labels and shuffled them in a pile. Laura found the label for knife and placed it on the knife.

Young Laura with Doctor Howe. Laura and all the blind students wore green silk ribbons around their heads because their eyes were often considered unattractive. (Perkins School for the Blind)

A pat from Doctor. A squeeze from Miss Drew. More smiles from Laura.

Finally, Laura worked with single raised letters on separate pieces of paper. Howe gave Laura the key, then mixed up the letters *K, E, Y.* Laura put the letters in the correct order.

Pat. Smile.

On the third day, like a wave crashing on the shore, Laura's breakthrough came. Neither Laura nor her teachers remembered the exact word later. But they recalled that her smile became a broad grin; her laughter, contagious. She threw her arms around her teachers, then rushed from object to object to name each with its label.

Howe wrote that all at once "the truth began to flash upon her—her intellect began to work—she perceived that here was a way by which she could herself make up a sign of anything that was in her own mind, and show it to another mind."

Words. Laura was dizzy with them!

Next Howe introduced Laura to a device he used with his other blind students—a set of twenty-six metal squares. Each, like the paper labels, had a letter of the alphabet raised so she could feel it. In the short space of a morning, Laura learned to arrange the letters in alphabetical order. Soon she felt an object, then spelled the word correctly with her squares.

A set of metal squares like the ones Laura used, each with a separate letter of the alphabet or a number on it. (Perkins School for the Blind, photo by Bruce Blakeslee)

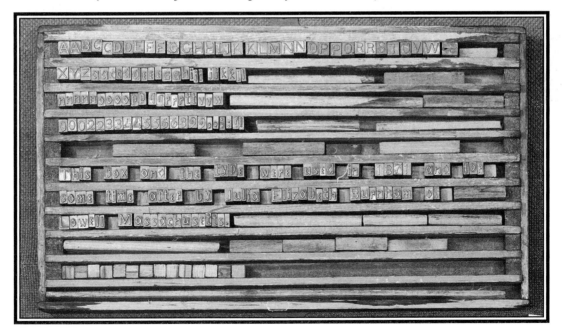

But Laura also needed to learn like deaf students, and that meant mastering fingerspelling, or the manual alphabet. She felt an apple Lydia Drew gave her and recognized it immediately. Then Miss Drew set up Laura's metal squares for the word "apple." Laura touched them and smiled. Next her teacher gave her only the metal square *A*. Then Laura had to feel the shape of Miss Drew's hand for the manual alphabet representation of the letter *A*—four fingers flat against the palm and thumb up, folded against the bent index finger. Carefully, she arranged her small fingers to match her teacher's.

"Think," she must have told herself. "And remember."

Presto! She learned the manual alphabet with amazing speed—in just a single afternoon. Lydia Drew patted Laura's head; Laura flung her arms around her.

Soon Laura's fingers were moving while she slept, spelling out the conversations in her dreams. And in no time, Laura spoke with her fingers as quickly as other people spoke with their voices.

Conversation—how thrilling! How astonishing! Laura had never been able to ask the questions all children ask: "What's this?" "What's that?" "Why?" She'd been through a long winter, but finally she budded, bloomed. Com-

The manual alphabet, also known as fingerspelling, can be used to communicate with a person who is Deaf-Blind. Words are fingerspelled into the palm of the person's hand, a process called "tactual fingerspelling." (Helen Keller National Center)

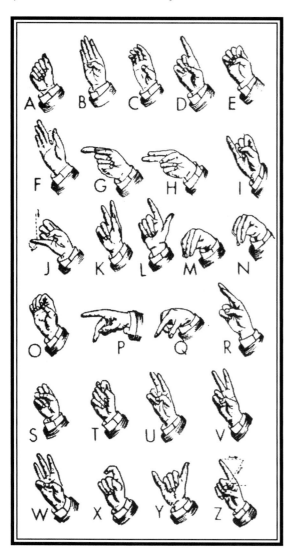

This is the word "touch" in sign language. Most educators in Howe's day approved of fingerspelling but not sign language. They denounced it as crude pantomime, even barbaric. Like Alexander Graham Bell, inventor of the telephone, and many others, Samuel Howe worried that deaf people who used signs would be separated from society. By the 1880s sign language was banned in the United States and Europe. But by 1900 many educators chose to teach it. The debate about teaching deaf people to sign or to speak still goes on today. (Model: Jessica Kurs-Lasky; photo by Bob Alexander.)

municating became all-important. She requested the name of every object she touched, the names of her forty female classmates. With hands outstretched in the hall, she felt the air's agitation and insisted on greeting each passerby, recognizing all by the vibrations of their footsteps, by the slightest contact with their hands or dresses. She taught other students the manual alphabet and forced them to talk to her, even when they didn't want to. But she dropped the hands of girls who were too slow to learn, and even snubbed some whose hands were dirty or "cold as a frog."

At dinner she demanded, "Bread give Laura." When Miss Drew gave her bread and turned to help another blind student, Laura, now a chatterbox, ordered, "Water drink Laura."

All day, all evening, Laura's fingers flashed. Miss Drew had no rest until Miss Chatterbox went to sleep.

8

Schoolgirl

Laura found words relatively late in her life, just before it became too late for her brain to grasp language fully. Today, experts believe children must be exposed to language before puberty if they are to communicate fluently. Otherwise, they will never speak more than a few individual words. Adults can learn a second language, although with more effort than children, only because their brains' language centers are already developed.

Laura learned words at eight years old. Helen Keller, another famous Deaf-Blind person born fifty years after Laura, understood language at seven.

Howe wasn't entirely aware of the effect age had on language learning. After his astounding success with Laura, he thought he'd found the formula for educating the Deaf-Blind. He brought Julia Brace and two new people, Lucy Reed and Oliver Caswell, to Perkins and tried to teach them. Since his efforts with Julia five years before, he'd changed his approach, using raised-print labels as a first step and introducing the manual alphabet later. But even with Laura working with them each day, Howe

Laura trying to teach her friend Oliver Caswell, who was also deaf and blind. (Perkins School for the Blind)

failed to reach Lucy or Julia. The third and youngest, Oliver Caswell, learned some nouns and verbs but never progressed enough to fingerspell in complete sentences. For instance, when he cut his finger on a dish, he spelled, "Cut dish."

Today, psychologists understand that Howe's methods weren't at fault. These three students simply tried to learn language too late in their lives. Lucy Reid was fourteen; Julia Brace, thirty-five; and Oliver, twelve. They were much older than Laura was when she was first introduced to language, and none of them had Laura's memory, curiosity, or remarkable intelligence.

Once Laura learned the concept of language, she began to attend regular classes at the Institution. With the exception of weekends and holidays, her daily schedule was as follows:

6:15–7:00 A.M.: Arithmetic

7:00–9:00 A.M.: Breakfast and domestic duties [Girls were required to make their beds, clean their rooms, and take care of their clothes at this time. Boys went outside to play.]

9:00–10:00 A.M.: Conversation with teacher, where Laura talked about anything on her mind—her favorite time

10:00–11:00 A.M.: Geography

A group of blind students pose in a classroom at Perkins. This photo was taken in 1893, so they are Helen Keller's contemporaries, not Laura's. (Perkins School for the Blind)

11:00 A.M.–12:00 noon: Writing

12:00 noon–1:00 P.M.: Reading to Laura, with conversation on the subjects

1:00–2:00 P.M.: Knitting and sewing

2:00–3:00 P.M.: Calisthenics with other blind girls [Howe felt that the blind were generally in poor physical shape and resolved to give them lots of physical exercise. He also remembered sitting for hours on hard benches in his own school days, and concluded that children needed physical as well as mental activity.]

3:00 P.M.: Dinner

After dinner: A five- to six-mile walk with teacher

After walk until 6:00 P.M.: Knitting

6:00 P.M.: Bedtime [In fact, the younger blind students went to bed closer to 7:00 P.M. The older students spent an hour after dinner singing and still another hour socializing. They went to bed closer to 9:00 P.M.]

The last fifteen minutes of each period was a recess.

The five- to six-mile walk along the streets of Boston proved to be another favorite part of Laura's school day. To Lydia Drew, it was the most difficult part. Laura leaned on Miss Drew's arm with most of her weight, her right hand moving nonstop with questions. Over the course of her first four years at the Institution, Laura's vocabulary grew, enabling her to pose very difficult questions:

"Why does it rain?"

"Why does our heart not stop?"

"Are there people on the Sun?"

"How do we know there is air?"

"What is wind made of?"

"Who made the water?"

During Laura's first years at the Institution the number of students grew, and the school moved to this building in South Boston. (Perkins School for the Blind)

"Do the words 'think,' 'guess,' 'suppose,' and 'understand' all mean the same?"

Miss Drew tried to watch where they were going, read Laura's dancing fingers, and spell back the answers into her pupil's hand. Most people would have had trouble answering Laura's questions even without also attempting to walk and guide her. But the questions always made Miss Drew think about the world in ways she wasn't accustomed to, especially when Laura stopped and insisted on knowing everything her teacher could see and hear at that particular location. Laura learned about the different jobs people had, about the various animals in her neighborhood, and about the foods in the market. This led to more questions:

"Do milliners make stockings?"

"Why did God not give animals souls?"

"Why are pineapples pine?"

Miss Drew came to realize that Laura was using her as an additional sense. She decided to explain to Laura that most people had five functioning senses but that she, Laura, had only one—touch—or at best, three. Sometimes Laura's senses of taste and smell worked, but she never put them to any use.

"I have four," Laura argued.

"Four what?"

"Four senses. Think, and nose, mouth, and fingers. I have four senses."

Miss Drew must have smiled. Laura certainly did have think!

9

Windows Open

Every day Laura came to Miss Drew with a list of words to define. And when the meaning of a word became clear to her, Laura laughed aloud and threw her arms around her teacher.

Laura loved playing tricks. Sometimes she purposely misspelled a word, and when Miss Drew corrected her, she burst into joyous laughter.

People entering a room or walking down the hall could not escape Laura; she always detected their vibrations. During lessons she grew restless if not allowed to greet a passerby. Conversations with other students steadily increased her vocabulary.

At the age of nine, after a year of instruction, her vocabulary was that of an ordinary three-year-old. But with all the stimulation and learning, her vocabulary quickly doubled and then tripled.

After working on nouns and verbs, Laura studied adjectives. She began the new lessons with familiar objects that had qualities she'd be able to feel, such as "wet" cloth or "dry" cloth, "bumpy" washboard, or "slippery" soap. Any adjectives that were based on the sense of touch, like "hard" and "heavy," were easy for Laura to understand.

But those related to the other senses were more difficult for her to grasp—colors, for example. Laura said that she'd like to have pink eyes and blue hair. She spoke of the "blue" roses and asked if horses were "green" and "blue" and "pink," knowing that they weren't. Her teachers said that occasionally she detected the color of a fabric from the surface that the dye had produced. Once she asked, "What color is think?"

She struggled to learn adjectives that had to do with taste or smell, such as "sweet," and those having to do with hearing, such as "loud." Laura enjoyed coining new words, such as "strongless" and "weakful" and "unremember." When her teacher explained that these weren't real words, Laura asked, "Why not?"

Miss Drew could only answer, "They just aren't."

In October 1839 Laura and Miss Drew paid a visit to Laura's family in Hanover. It had been two years since she had left home. A hand stroked Laura's hair—one she knew well. But she didn't have a name for its owner.

"Father," her teacher spelled.

Laura repeated the word, and a fog lifted—her spirit, too.

A year before, Harmony had visited Laura in Boston. At that time, Miss Drew had taught Laura the word "Mother." Now, inside the farmhouse, she found Mother again and sprang to her arms. Then more familiar hands and arms and people of differing sizes, shapes, and textures greeted Laura.

"Brother," "Addison," "John," Miss Drew spelled.

In Laura's mind, a window opened, and delight floated in.

She pulled her teacher from room to room, to every object, so familiar, yet unnamed. She was especially interested in the loom and the spinning wheel, which she'd felt her mother use so often. Then she led Miss Drew to the beehive and asked for its name. One by one, objects were identified with her newly discovered vocabulary. Soon all became hers.

Then Laura returned to her mother and began teaching her the manual alphabet. She placed her small fingers around Harmony's hand and moved her mother's fingers in the correct positions. As Harmony caught on, Laura hugged her.

By this time Laura had become shy around men, except for Doctor. Her teacher worried that she would reject her father and Mr. Tenney, but Laura seemed just as affectionate as before. She wandered off with Uncle Asa as she'd always done.

After two weeks, when it was time to return to Boston, Miss Drew expected Laura to resist and put up a fuss. The year before, when Harmony's visit to Boston came to an end, Laura had clung to her mother, then had fallen against a school matron, sobbing. But this time Laura parted from her family very calmly.

Back at school, Laura fell in love with reading.

Doctor "had a little book entitled *A Child's Book* raised in blind letters," Laura later wrote. "He taught me how to read the words with my own finger. I was so very fond of reading."

Laura wasn't quite so fond of some other subjects, though. In June 1840, when she was ten and a half, she began learning arithmetic. First, she studied how to add, then how to subtract, using a special metal case developed for the blind students. In just nine days, she learned to add a column of numbers totaling thirty, such as seven plus four plus five plus eight plus six. But if she wanted to refer to a number greater than she knew how to count, she always spelled "one hundred." When she thought a person would be absent for many years, she said "Will come hundred Sundays," meaning one hundred weeks.

After she'd become skillful in adding and subtracting, Laura began multiplication, which she considered her most "irksome" subject.

"If you think, you will understand," her teacher told her.

This photo shows a metal case similar to the one Laura used for arithmetic.
(Perkins School for the Blind, photo by Bruce Blakeslee)

Laura spelled out, "My think is very tired."

The teacher replied, "I will have to tell Doctor or write this in my journal."

Laura begged her not to. She promised to try harder. She still had a deep curiosity, but sometimes when the material was hard, her interest faded. However, her teachers could almost always persuade her to keep trying by bringing up Dr. Howe's name. Laura never wanted to disappoint him or lose his approval.

Writing was another class that annoyed Laura. She folded a piece of paper in half and slid a piece of pasteboard inside. The pasteboard had grooved straight lines about an inch apart. Through the paper, Laura could feel the grooves and use them as a guide to write straight across the page. Next, her teacher used a pin to prick the outline of a letter on a piece of stiff paper so that Laura might feel its shape. Then the teacher guided Laura's right hand to help her reproduce it with a pencil. Undoubtedly, Laura failed to write the letters legibly at times.

But how could she know? Why should she care?

Crossing *t*'s, writing *x*'s, and dotting *i*'s proved difficult. She often lost her place within the word. And she couldn't double-check what she had written.

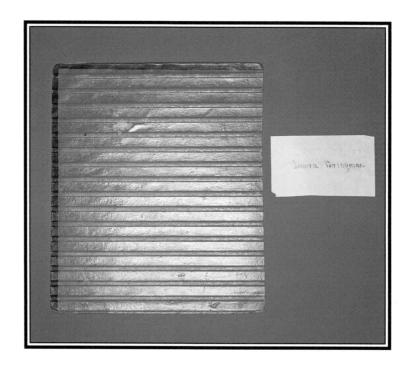

This is the pasteboard device with raised lines that Laura used for writing. (Perkins School for the Blind, photo by Bruce Blakeslee)

laura will write
letter to mother
laura will ride
with father. laura
will go to house
for another laura
will abide with
mother and father
mother will love
and live. laura now
laura will carry
letter for mother
laura will go to school.
laura will go home.

Laura wrote this, her first letter, late in 1839, when she was 10 years old. (Perkins School for the Blind, photo by Bruce Blakeslee)

At first, writing these letters seemed pointless! Eventually, though, Laura mastered writing, and her teacher observed that when "at last the idea dawned upon her, that by this mysterious process she could make other people understand what she thought, her joy was boundless."

10

Weapon or Masterpiece?

Over the years Howe expanded his efforts to improve education for all young people, not just for Laura and other disabled children. He became so busy that Laura spent most of her learning time with Miss Drew.

Teachers all over New England were arguing about the best way to educate students. Most believed in the notion of "original sin," which held that children were born with the tendency to misbehave because of Adam and Eve's disobedience in the Garden of Eden, as told in the Bible. Therefore, teachers thought they should bully and scare their students—even beat the sin out of them. Children were innately sinful, and they learned best from the strongest teacher: fear.

Doctor disagreed. So did the man who became known as the "Father of the Common Schools" (elementary schools), Horace Mann. Howe and Mann had unusual educational ideas for their time. They claimed that all children were as good and curious and eager to learn as Laura—and she had never been spanked. They argued that children should learn from joy and from experience, just like Laura, who, they claimed, was "pure as Eve." This assertion was a bit of an exaggeration, of course. Like

Horace Mann (1796–1859) worked for education in Massachusetts and established a model for the country's elementary school system. In 1839 he created the first school to train teachers, in Lexington, Massachusetts. Several of Laura's teachers graduated from it. (Library of Congress)

all children, Laura could be rebellious. But she always regretted her outbursts of anger and couldn't rest until people forgave her.

Every time Howe argued with other teachers, he brought up Laura and her successes. She was his best weapon against his opponents, who accused him of being a "wild schemer, using a child's education only to promote his own . . . theory." But Howe's theory worked; Laura and all his blind students responded to a demanding but kind teacher. And his techniques withstood the test of time. Fifty years later, Anne Sullivan, who

Anne Sullivan Macy (1866–1936) was the daughter of poor Irish immigrants. At the age of five, a disease made her almost blind. Two years later, her mother died, and Anne and her brother were sent to a workhouse by their alcoholic father. Anne then went to Perkins School, had two operations that restored most of her sight, and graduated as valedictorian of her class in 1886. (Perkins School for the Blind)

learned to fingerspell from Laura, studied Howe's methods and used them with her famous Deaf-Blind pupil, Helen Keller. And indeed, Howe's methods are still used with Deaf-Blind people today.

In 1840, when Laura was ten and a half, Howe declared his experiment of teaching her a complete victory. Many people around the country had come to know of Laura through Howe's yearly written reports to the Massachusetts state legislature. These accounts of Laura and the other blind students captured their imaginations. Soon, people began referring to her as an educational masterpiece. Laura, the dependent child saved by education, was proof that anyone could conquer challenges and learn.

Laura deserved every praiseworthy label. By the time she reached her eleventh birthday, she'd become a symbol and a model for others. But her teachers didn't tell her about the praise and impressive titles, so she remained unaware of them. Laura learned because she loved to do so, and because she wasn't bullied or scared.

More than fame or fancy labels, she wanted someone beside her, a companion. And with Howe spending less and less time with her, she grew even more attached to the caring Lydia Drew. But in late October 1841, a few weeks after Laura and Miss Drew had again visited the Bridgmans in Hanover, Laura's beloved teacher resigned to get married.

Throughout the 1800s women were not allowed to continue teaching once they married. So Laura "had the grief of parting with her old and much-loved teacher," someone she'd been with more intensely than her parents or anyone else.

"I was very strongly attached to her," Laura wrote in her memoir.

Lydia Drew invited Laura for a visit just two months later and hosted her occasionally for the rest of her life, but Laura missed their daily contact. No one ever joked with Laura or appreciated her sense of humor as much as Lydia Drew did.

Howe didn't find another teacher for Laura for four months. Finally, in February 1842 he hired Mary Swift, who taught Laura for two hours a day. Another teacher, Eliza Rogers, instructed her for an additional hour. This meant that Laura passed lots of time by herself, and time alone proved to be more difficult for her than for other children.

As the minutes ticked by, Laura wondered what was happening to Miss Swift. Where was she? Sometimes Miss Swift met with Doctor or rested. Other times she was simply busy.

Laura's right hand made up conversations with her left. If she made a mistake, she swatted her speaking hand with her other hand, just as her teacher did. But eventually, boredom set in. No new books. No companionship.

But wait! Finally, she felt her teacher's footsteps in the air, felt her touch.

"Where were you?" Laura asked. "I was afraid some bad people or wild animals had killed you."

Laura tried to fill her hours of solitude. She knitted, sewed, crocheted, read, and wrote letters, some even in French. Still, her response to a lesson on the word "alone" summed up her dislike of these solitary hours.

Here is fourteen-year-old Laura with one of her teachers. The teacher's identity is uncertain. The photo was taken in 1845, the year Mary Swift stopped teaching Laura and Sarah Wight began. Probably this is Sarah Wight, who worked with Laura until 1851. Laura grew to love Sarah Wight as much as she had loved Lydia Drew, referring to Wight as "my dearest teacher."
(Perkins School for the Blind)

After Laura learned the meaning of "alone," her teacher told her to go somewhere by herself, or *a-l-o-n-e*. Wanting, instead, to go with a friend, Laura replied that she wanted to go *"al-two."*

But "al-two" wasn't always possible at Perkins, or even during her infrequent visits home. In 1842, just following Laura's twelfth birthday, Harmony Bridgman had another child named Mary, after Laura's sister who had died. And over the next few years Harmony had two more daughters, Collina, named after the other sister who had died, and Ellen, called Nellie. Harmony became busier than ever and couldn't provide the constant company that Laura sought. Laura's brother Addison learned a little fingerspelling, but he had his studies and his chores and little time to spend with Laura.

Mary Swift and the teacher who replaced her in 1845, Sarah Wight, found it exhausting to work with Laura nonstop. Still, now that Howe's methods had worked and Laura could communicate, she prized companionship over all else.

11

"Is God Ever Surprised?"

Doctor says I am to love God," Laura wrote often in her journal. And from her earliest days at Perkins, she did.

Just as there was much debate about education in New England in the 1830s and 1840s, there was also plenty of discussion about religion. "The Bible is the true word of God," most people said. "The Bible was inspired by God—but written by humans and therefore open to mistakes," others countered.

Once again, Howe referred to Laura and her story in developing his own arguments.

When Laura came to Perkins, she didn't have any religious ideas at all. Still, Howe saw her as highly moral, even though she was untaught. He wrote, "Few children are so affectionate or so . . . conscientious. Few are so sensible of their own rights or regardful of the rights of others. She is always eager to share with others and to take care of sick people. She has a keen sensitivity to people with disabilities."

One exception was her treatment of children who were slower to learn than most. Laura ignored them or, worse, made them wait on her. Even though most of her information came from open-minded adults, she somehow absorbed the idea that, of all the disabilities, mental retardation carried the biggest social stigma and was the least acceptable handicap. Although many blind students felt superior to Laura because she had two disabilities while they had only one, Laura felt superior to the children at Perkins who were considered "feeble-minded."

Despite this attitude, Howe thought Laura possessed unusual honesty and decency. Instead of telling her outright what to believe, he hoped she would develop the notion of a loving God all by herself. He wanted her to learn about creation in nature by feeling seeds grow into vegetables. Eventually, he thought, she would begin to form an idea of a creator of all life.

Howe was a Unitarian. He believed in God but didn't think that God had three natures (Father, Son, and Holy Spirit). He didn't believe that Jesus was both divine and human at the same time—just human. And he rejected the concept of original sin. He believed that human beings were born with good, not sinful, natures and that good behavior could lead them eventually to heaven.

Howe guided Laura's religious education. He allowed her to socialize only with students who believed as he did, and he forbade the teachers from telling her about different religious views.

During her lessons, Laura thought of many religious questions. But when she raised them, her teachers told her to ask Doctor. For instance, once the teacher Eliza Rogers found Laura reading the Book of Psalms and looking pale. "God is angry with the wicked every day. I was angry this year and last year, and I deceived Swift many times."

Miss Rogers diverted Laura from the subject, but later Laura returned to the topic with Miss Swift.

"God will judge all people. What is 'judge'?"

Miss Swift told Laura that she couldn't understand all of Psalms just then, but when Dr. Howe came home, he would teach her more.

Another time, Laura asked, "Why do you not teach me as Doctor does about the Bible?"

Sarah Wight explained that she and Dr. Howe didn't "think exactly alike about all things."

"Why not?" asked Laura. She seemed troubled. Doctor's authority had always been absolute. This was probably the first time Laura realized there could be views different from those of Howe.

But soon she turned to other questions.

"Is there a door to the Heaven?"

"How large is heaven?"

"Does God know Latin?"

"Is God ever surprised?"

"Does God know as much as Doctor?"

And about herself she wondered: "Why do I have two thoughts [right and wrong]? And why do I not do what my conscience tells me is right?"

As concerned as she was about being right and good, Laura didn't always behave perfectly. She had a quick temper, and once she hit a student. Afterward, she said, "I will go home and come no more."

When asked why, she said, "Because I cannot be good in Boston."

"Your mother will be sorry if you are naughty," her teacher said.

"My mother will love me," Laura contradicted.

"Are you sorry you came to Boston?"

"No," she said. "Because I could not talk with fingers when I came with my father and mother."

"If you go home and come no more, you can talk with no one with fingers."

"My mother will talk *little slow.*"

Laura longed to have more friends. Occasionally, the blind girls played

This is the Book of Psalms in raised print that Laura used.
(Perkins School for the Blind, photos by Bruce Blakeslee)

with her, but most of them resented her because she lived with Doctor in his apartment. If she had lived in the dormitories, she might have made closer ties. Sometimes Laura's desire to interact with others drove her to misbehave. Once, she didn't want to stop playing with her friend Sophia and go to her lesson, so she lied and said that the teacher had gone to downtown Boston. When confronted, she apologized and said she wouldn't tell any more lies, but she still wondered why the teacher had made her leave Sophia.

So Laura wasn't as saintly as Howe claimed in his reports to the legislature, but she always wanted to be good. She sometimes actually slapped herself for doing something wrong. "My left hand harmed me," she said.

Laura liked thinking about good and evil. She amazed her teachers with her ability to think of abstract ideas like God, love, right, wrong. Oliver Caswell and other Deaf-Blind students struggled to understand concrete concepts like chair and table.

Although Howe tried, he couldn't control Laura's contact with different religious beliefs. As time passed, her teachers couldn't resist sharing their opinions that differed from Howe's. Through conversations with them and the other blind girls, Laura learned about the concept of Hell. The idea scared her.

But she also learned about Heaven and about God being always present. These ideas comforted her.

In the time she spent alone, Laura often read the raised-print version of the New Testament, as well as the Book of Psalms, and prayed. Soon she considered God her most constant companion, the faithful friend she'd always sought. It was through her religious faith that she found consolation, the solution to her loneliness.

12

Famous

Dr. Howe put the blind students on exhibit at the Institution every Saturday to raise awareness of what blind people could do, but also to raise money. As early as February 1840 Laura took part in these events. Soon, hundreds of spectators were coming to see her. In front of each audience, Laura performed. She found mountains on relief maps or little-known places, like the Canary Islands, on an enormous globe that measured thirteen feet ten inches in circumference. She read from her book and fingerspelled to her teacher, who interpreted. She showed onlookers how she wrote using a regular pencil and paper. She added and subtracted numbers. She fascinated the audience, who pressed in around her, and she completely stole the show.

Soon Laura was the biggest tourist attraction in Boston. In 1841, 1842, and 1843 she reached the height of her fame. Parents all over the United States held her up as an example to their children. Teachers reminded reluctant students to compare their own efforts with those of the young deaf and blind girl who had accomplished so much in spite of such overwhelming obstacles.

This is the large tactile globe that Laura used in her geography classes and when performing before audiences at the Institution. It was made by Stephen Preston Ruggles in 1837. According to the Perkins Museum website, the globe is about 53 inches tall "and consists of some 700 pieces of wood glued together so well that no cracks have ever shown up." (Perkins School for the Blind, photo by Bruce Blakeslee)

"You must try harder," they said. "Remember little Laura Bridgman and the difficulties she faces."

Laura's fame even spread across the ocean. In February 1842 Charles Dickens visited Laura in Boston and was immediately enchanted. He likened her to Little Nell, the heroine in his book *The Old Curiosity Shop.*

"Her face was radiant with intelligence and pleasure. Her hair, braided by her own hands, was bound about" her head, Dickens wrote. "Her dress, arranged by herself, was a pattern of neatness and simplicity; the work she had knitted, lay beside her; her writing-book was on the desk she leaned upon. . . . Like other inmates of that house, she had a green ribbon bound round her eyelids. A doll she had dressed lay near upon the ground."

Dickens devoted a whole chapter to Laura in his book *American Notes.* Forty years later, Kate Adams Keller read the book and discovered that her daughter, Helen, could be helped.

The renowned scientist Charles Darwin also wrote about Laura in his book *The Descent of Man, and Selection in Relation to Sex.* The American reformer Dorothea Dix offered money to support Laura's education. Sophia Peabody, the wife of author Nathaniel Hawthorne, received a commission from Samuel Gridley Howe and sculpted a bust of Laura in September 1841. Other famous reformers, poets, and artists

Charles Darwin (1809–82) is best known for his groundbreaking theory of evolution. In The Descent of Man *Darwin uses Laura as an example to prove his theory that language is necessary for thought: "even an ordinary train of thought almost requires . . . some form of language, for . . . Laura Bridgman, was observed to use her fingers while dreaming . . ." (Library of Congress)*

flocked to meet her, to find hope and inspiration. All requested her autograph.

Newspapers reported that she was the most famous person in the United States. At the time, only Queen Victoria of England was more celebrated. Yet Laura certainly didn't insist on being with all the celebrities of her day, just the "best-dressed," whose clothing felt soft and pleasant to her hand.

Though Howe tried to keep the public's admiring words from her, Laura did have some sense of the attention she drew. When Howe worried that the crush of bodies encircling her during the exhibits could risk her

Laura's autograph was a collector's item in the 1840s.
(Perkins School for the Blind)

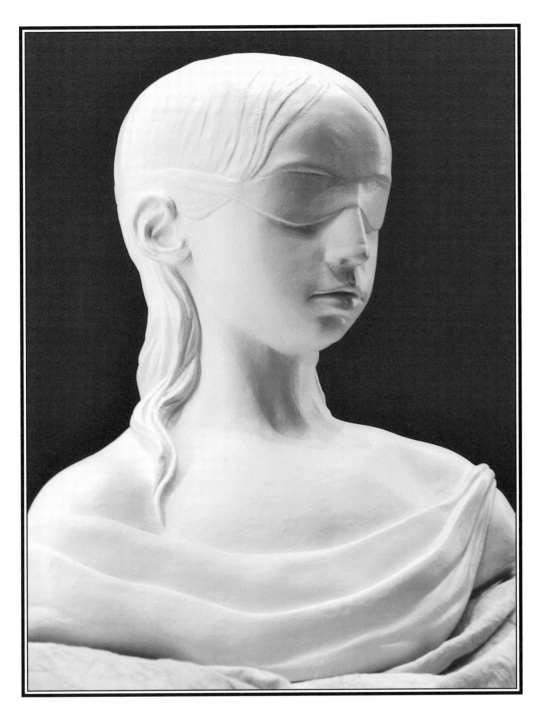

Sophia Peabody was so impressed with Laura that she agreed to sculpt this bust of her. Peabody was married to Nathaniel Hawthorne (1804–64), author of the novel The Scarlet Letter *and many short stories. (Perkins School for the Blind, photo by Bruce Blakeslee)*

This is a picture of Helen Keller (1880–1968) as an adult, with her teacher, Anne Sullivan Macy (standing). Helen became deaf and blind at the age of nineteen months. Unlike Laura, Helen retained her senses of smell and taste. With Anne's help, Helen learned to speak with her fingers, to read raised print and Braille, and to write with pen and paper as well as with a Braillewriter and a regular typewriter. She graduated from Radcliffe College, wrote many books, and worked tirelessly for the well-being of blind and disabled people. (Perkins School for the Blind)

safety, he had benches placed as barriers to keep back the crowd. Following the next exhibition, Laura complained, "Are ladies afraid of me?" She thought the barricades protected the people from her rather than the other way around.

So she did enjoy the throng, the many vibrations, the excitement. She relished the proud touches of her teachers, of Doctor. To Laura, fame meant company, other people, excitement. Not being alone.

Scholars in many fields—education, psychology, philosophy—praised Samuel Gridley Howe's work with Laura. In the mid-1800s he received as much admiration as "the miracle worker," Anne Sullivan, would receive in the 1900s for her work with Helen Keller.

Laura became a symbol of the power of educational techniques to transform seemingly hopeless cases. She was living proof that everyone should be given an equal chance. Because of her courage and intelligence in the face of such great challenges, she represented hope and possibility for all people, no matter their circumstances. Little Laura Bridgman from Hanover, New Hampshire, had captured everyone's attention. She had touched the world.

13

Farewells

On April 23, 1843, when Laura was at the height of her fame, Doctor married. He and his wife, Julia Ward, went to Europe for an eighteen-month honeymoon and speaking tour.

"Does Doctor love me like Julia?" Laura asked Miss Swift eight months later.

"No," she replied.

"Does he love God like Julia?"

Miss Swift spelled, "Yes."

When the Howes returned in September 1844, Laura's familiar life at Perkins changed. They came home from Europe with a six-month-old baby, Julia Romana. Laura had to move out of the apartment she'd shared with Doctor and his sister Jeannette for seven years and into the girls' dormitory. Her closest associate, Miss Swift, left to marry a year later. Sarah Wight, who replaced Miss Swift, resigned in 1851, also to marry. Laura always yearned to marry or to keep house for her brother Addison or her teachers, but it was not to be.

After 1851 Howe stopped assigning a teacher or companion for Laura.

Samuel Gridley Howe as a middle-aged man. (Perkins School for the Blind)

Although he still directed the Perkins School and still cared about Laura, he grew more involved in other causes.

Laura continued to visit her family for short vacations, but the Bridgmans were always too busy with chores and other demands to give Laura the stimulation she needed. Uncle Asa spent time with her, but he never learned the manual alphabet. On Laura's seventeenth birthday, December 21, 1846, he died.

Without sufficient stimulation or regular companionship in Hanover, Laura decided to make Perkins her permanent home. She busied herself by helping to wake the girls, by cleaning, by teaching sewing, and by acting generally as the school's "house assistant," a kind of voluntary Cinderella. Always, she read and wrote letters. Words—those in the Bible, in other books, in letters and conversation—words, so hard to learn, sustained and comforted her.

Occasionally, she visited with Howe, but he spent more and more time away from the school, working tirelessly to abolish slavery, helping Dorothea Dix improve insane asylums and prison conditions. During the Civil War, 1861–65, Howe worked for the federal sanitation department. After the war he helped to educate freed slaves.

In January 1876 Julia Ward Howe called Laura to Doctor's bedside, as he lay dying of a brain tumor. Someone placed her hand on Howe's forehead, warm and moist with perspiration.

Dorothea Dix (1802–87) was a philanthropist and reformer who made improving conditions for people with mental illness and people in prison her life's work. She believed that all people—whether they were disabled, like Laura, or mentally ill or imprisoned—deserved fair treatment and equal opportunity. (Library of Congress)

Laura at about age nineteen or twenty. (Perkins School for the Blind)

"They consented for me to kiss him farewell," Laura recorded in her journal.

Howe left money in his will for Laura, making her financially independent.

Laura wrote about her "best earthly friend and greatest benefactor," saying, "I think much of Dr. H. day and night with sorrow, and gratitude, and love, and sincerity."

People referred to him as her "spiritual" father, the one who had

Here is Laura as an adult, seated at a sewing machine. (Perkins School for the Blind)

Julia Ward Howe (1819–1910), the wife of Samuel Gridley Howe, shared in his work with Laura and other blind students. A prominent abolitionist, she wrote the poem "Battle Hymn of the Republic," which was set to music and became the most popular song of the Civil War. After the war, Julia Ward Howe focused her energies on women's suffrage and, for the rest of her life, fought for women's rights. (Library of Congress)

granted her a second chance at life. But to Laura, he had been her "dearly beloved and adopted father."

Michael Anagnos, who had married Howe's daughter Julia Romana, took over the running of Perkins. Throughout the 1880s Laura helped him, going out in public to raise money for her favorite project, a kindergarten for blind children. Even in her fifties, she could still impress a crowd.

On Laura's fifty-eighth birthday, December 21, 1887, the Perkins School celebrated her fiftieth anniversary there. Julia Ward Howe led the jubilee celebration, reading a short speech Laura had written. The blind kindergartners, who owed much to Laura for their educational opportunity, sang to her.

She wrote to her mother, "I am so highly honored with kind

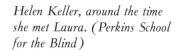

Helen Keller, around the time she met Laura. (Perkins School for the Blind)

remembrances from friends and strangers, according to my anniversary reception."

In May 1888 Laura met the eight-year-old Deaf-Blind girl that people were calling "the new Laura Bridgman." Her name was Helen Keller. Years before, Laura had taught Helen's teacher, Anne Sullivan, a Perkins student, to fingerspell. Laura found Anne's remarkable pupil poorly behaved and wild.

"You have not taught her to be very gentle," Laura scolded.

Soon after this encounter, Laura's health began to fail. In a letter to her mother dated February 1889 Laura wrote: "I have felt poorly and weakly a great part of this winter. . . . I was ill sometimes. My throat was thorny and sore for two weeks, too. . . . I get tired quickly."

She complained of dizziness and held her head, as if in pain. Her friends grew worried about her in late April 1889.

"Pneumonia," the doctor said.

At the age of eighty-five, her mother was unable to make the long trip to Boston to be with her sick daughter. But Laura's sisters Collina and Nellie sat with her at her bedside. Gradually, she grew very weak. On May 24, 1889, Laura tried to spell something and managed to make four letters, *"Moth—."*

"Mother?" a school matron asked with her fingers.

Laura simply nodded. Then, three hours later, she was gone.

Afterword

◆ ◆ ◆ ◆ ◆ ◆ ◆ ◆ ◆ ◆ ◆ ◆ ◆ ◆ ◆ ◆ ◆ ◆ ◆ ◆

IF LAURA WERE ALIVE TODAY

When you think of someone deaf and blind, you usually picture a person who's completely without vision or hearing, like Laura. But most of the 70,000 to 100,000 Deaf-Blind people in the United States today have some hearing or some sight or a little bit of both.

Sally Alexander, the coauthor of this book, is totally blind and partially deaf.

I, more than Laura, represent today's Deaf-Blind community. When I lost my sight, at the age of twenty-six, I heard about the remarkable accomplishments of Laura Bridgman. As I began to have hearing problems a year later, her story of challenge and triumph took on new meaning for me.

People often praise me for my courage and humor in performing the tasks of ordinary life—cooking, cleaning, errand-running, teaching, and parenting—but I know I face many fewer difficulties than Laura did. Although, like Laura, I am totally blind, and touch is a primary sense for me, I have sufficient, functioning hearing, improved by hearing aids. I am able to speak and smell and taste. Smell, like taste, provides pleasure—but it also offers enormous practical help. With my nose I can detect anything burning on my stove (or elsewhere). Outside of my home, I can identify my location by the smells coming from coffee shops,

Coauthor Sally Alexander and her guide dog, Ursula, at Laura's tombstone, which is located near the old Bridgman farmhouse, just outside Hanover, New Hampshire. (Photo by Bob Alexander)

pizza places, dry cleaners, bakeries, and gas stations. Most important, I benefit from living in the twenty-first century, with all its advances in law, medicine, education, social attitudes, and technology.

If Laura were alive today, she would have many more opportunities to lead an independent, full life. Her teachers would introduce her to Braille, sign language, and a Braille computer, but otherwise they would teach her exactly as her beloved Doctor did. The basic education of Deaf-Blind people today hasn't changed. The pioneering work done with Laura still touches the lives of all twenty-first-century Deaf-Blind people. What *has* changed since Laura's time are the laws, the medical practices, the attitudes toward people with disabilities, and the technology.

Laws: Laws have been passed since Laura lived that have opened doors to education and employment for Deaf-Blind people. The Americans with Disabilities Act, passed in 1990 and enacted on July 26, 1992, requires that people with disabilities are given access to materials, interpreting services, and equipment in schools and the workplace.

Medical Practices: Scarlet fever and many other diseases are treatable today with antibiotics, surgery, and medical procedures. If these had been available in Laura's time, she might not have lost both her sight and hearing from the disease. Today, many deaf people can have some hearing restored by medical procedures such as cochlear implants. A cochlear implant is an electronic hearing device that can help provide a sense of sound to someone who is deaf or severely hard-of-hearing.

For people with some sight, there are also many medical procedures to improve vision. Unfortunately, Laura would have needed entirely new eyes. So far, there isn't any surgery to transplant the whole eye, so nothing could have restored Laura's sight.

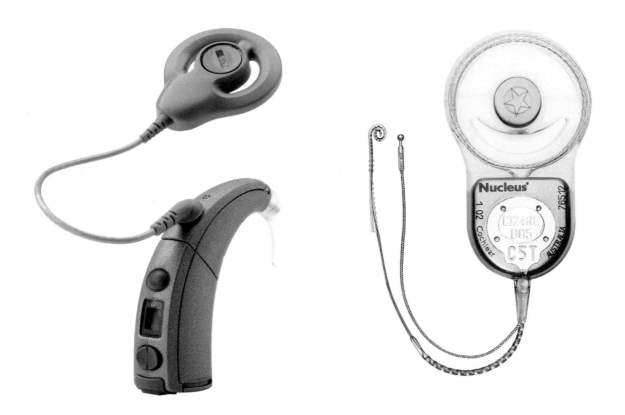

These two images show the external and internal parts of the cochlear implant. The picture on the left shows the parts that are worn outside the ear. First, sound goes into a microphone in the hooked object, which is worn behind the ear. A signal then goes through the cord into the circular object, which fits against the head above the ear. This circular object contains a magnet and is held in place on the head by a second magnet implanted under the skin. On the right are the implanted parts. The magnet under the skin is attached to a receiver, which transmits the signal through a cord. The curly end of the cord is placed carefully within the cochlea, deep in the ear. Here the ear receives the signal and transmits it to the brain, which "hears" the electrical signal as sound. The straight wire is a ground. It carries excess electricity away from the ear. (Cochlear Americas)

Attitudes: Attitudes toward people like Laura are more positive today. People in the United States see the disabled in schools, in public places, in the media, and in everyday situations. They may have seen TV footage of Erik Weihenmayer, a blind man, climbing Mt. Everest; of Bill Irwin hiking the 2,167-mile-long Appalachian Trail with his Seeing Eye dog, Orient. They are familiar with the blind actor Tom Sullivan and the deaf actor

Marlee Matlin, and the blind singers Stevie Wonder and the late Ray Charles. Some may have heard of the poet and memoirist Robert Smithdas, first Deaf-Blind person to earn both a bachelor's and a master's degree. They may not know of Scott Stoffel, a Federal Aviation Administration engineer who, while in college, invented a communication device for other Deaf-Blind individuals, but they expect that most people with disabilities can perform well in school and at work. Although Laura was told that she would not be permitted to marry, Deaf-Blind people today can marry and enjoy a life very much like everyone else. Again, Dr. Howe's breakthrough work with Laura created a shift in the public's views—proving that people who are severely disabled often have active minds and deserve education, not just training to do simple repetitive jobs.

Technology: Once Laura made it clear that the Deaf-Blind could be educated, and once people's attitudes changed to allow equal opportunities, the necessary technology was developed. Today, technological advances allow the Deaf-Blind and all disabled people much more independence. Those with some hearing can usually be helped by small but complex hearing aids and amplifiers. Those with some sight can use the many excellent magnification systems available to enhance what they see, such as non-illuminated and illuminated hand magnifiers; electronic magnifiers, commonly called CCTVs (closed circuit televisions); microscopic, prism, or telemicroscopic glasses; and lamp magnifiers. Another device, which is still too expensive for most people, is a voice-synthesized computer that looks like a digital camera. It takes a picture of any print material and converts it into speech for the owner to listen to.

If Laura were alive today, she would start her day with some fairly simple technology: an under-the-pillow vibrating attachment to a tactile alarm clock—a regular clock, without the crystal, that she could feel. The numbers 3, 6, 9, and 12 on the face of the clock would have two raised dots to help Laura know where the hands were pointing. Once in the bathroom, she would identify shampoo, toothpaste, deodorant, and other products by the container's shape or by Braille labels she'd already placed on them. She might go online, using a computer with a Braille display, to find out the weather forecast so she could dress appropriately. She could make telephone calls using special software on her computer. The call would go online to a relay service. She would type in the telephone number, and if that person didn't have a teletypewriter system (TTY), the relay person would voice everything that Laura said. The relay operator would type into the system the person's response, and Laura would read it on her computer's Braille display. When she felt hungry, Laura could cook, using a Braille overlay from an appliance company or Braille labels that she placed on the pad of her microwave or oven range herself. Many appliances have dials; Laura could also memorize the number of clicks for each setting.

When it was time to leave for work or to run errands, Laura could phone a paratransit system or a support-service driver. Many Deaf-Blind people today use guide dogs and travel independently on public buses or subways. On the Internet, they find maps and research beforehand the route they must take. They often carry a notetaker with Global Positioning System and read the Braille information about their route as they walk.

If Laura had to meet with someone who did not know how to fingerspell or sign, she could bring along a device called a screen Braille communicator. One side of the machine, which the nondisabled person would use, has a typewriter keyboard with an LCD screen. On the other side, facing the Deaf-Blind person, is a Braille keyboard and a small Braille display for reading. Everything that Laura Brailled on her side of the device would show up on the other person's screen in print. Everything that person typed would appear in Braille on Laura's display.

To relax, Laura might read Braille books, play chess or dominoes with special tactile marks, or have a game of Braille Scrabble. She could play cards or various board games using commercially Brailled sets.

And Laura could find work that would make her financially independent. At Perkins, she brought in a little money through the sale of her handiwork, but she relied on her inheritance from Dr. Howe for her support. Laura assisted the Perkins sewing teachers, but she never held a major teaching role. She probably taught Anne Sullivan and others the manual alphabet for her own personal reasons, and not as their official instructor.

A screen Braille communicator. (Photo by Chris Lagarde)

The Braille Scrabble set features a board with both print and Braille abbreviations, such as "TW" for triple word and "DL" for double letter. The letter squares feature both embossed print and Braille letters. The set includes Braille instructions. (Photo by Jim Greenburg)

Deaf-Blind people today work as teachers, engineers, counselors, computer programmers, office assistants, Braille transcriptionists, consultants, and more. Because most Deaf-Blind individuals have some hearing and/or sight, some even work as musicians or graphic designers. As with people who can see and hear, the job possibilities for the Deaf-Blind vary according to the person's interests and skills.

If Laura were alive today, she would live richly and independently, sharing with everyone the motto she'd learned from Dr. Howe, the motto she embraced throughout her life 150 years ago:

"Obstacles are things to be overcome."

Laura as an older woman. (Perkins School for the Blind)

Source Notes

Complete bibliographic information for books cited in the Source Notes can be found in the Bibliography, which starts on page 94.

Important People in Laura Bridgman's Life

p. ix Milo Bridgman was born November 2, 1838, after Laura had already moved to Perkins, and he died on April 2, 1839, of scarlet fever. It's doubtful that Laura ever met him. Edmund C. Sanford's transcription of Laura's 1849 autobiography, *The Writings of Laura Bridgman,* has one of the few references to Milo, on page 14.

1 A Delicate Plant

p. 1 The idea that Laura was a "delicate plant" comes from page 31 of Maud Howe Elliot and Florence Howe Hall's book, *Laura Bridgman: Dr. Howe's Famous Pupil and What He Taught Her.* Laura reminded Samuel Gridley Howe of a delicate plant. He wrote that she promised great ability and beauty but that her health might make it difficult for her to live "to maturity." However, Collina Bridgman Simmons denied that Laura had severe "fits." See Elisabeth Gitter, *The Imprisoned Guest: Samuel Howe and Laura Bridgman, the Original Deaf-Blind Girl,* page 287.

p. 3 There is some question today whether Laura and her sisters really suffered from scarlet fever. Gitter, page 300, note 8, suggests that her illness may have been meningitis, an inflammation of the membranes that cover the brain and spinal cord. This disease often results in a skin rash and a painful reaction to light, two of the symptoms Laura complained of. A professor of the history of medicine at the University of Pittsburgh, Dr. Jonathon Erlen, thinks the illness might have been encephalitis, an inflammation of the brain. But no definitive diagnosis has ever been made.

Today the two most common causes of Deaf-Blindness are congenital rubella and Usher's syndrome. If a woman is exposed to rubella, also known as German measles, during the first three months of her pregnancy, the baby can be born with vision and hearing problems. Usher's syndrome results in hearing loss combined with retinitis pigmentosa, a progressive eye disease that narrows the vision until just the center or tunnel vision is left.

p. 3   "I was saturated . . .": Sanford, page 8.

p. 4   "dark.": Gitter, page 46.

p. 5   "book": Gitter, page 46.

2 In Touch

p. 11   "I had a man's large boot . . .": Sanford, page 10.

3 Friend and Frustrations

p. 12   "Mr. Tenney was one of my greatest . . .": Sanford, page 14.

p. 12   "My dearest friend, Mr. Tenney, gave me . . .": The plate that Asa Tenney gave Laura would have had the print letters of the alphabet raised above its surface. It was probably not an educational tool but rather a novel way to decorate a plate. Sanford, page 9.

p. 15   "Those who cannot be 'taught' by reason . . .": Charles Dickens, *American Notes,* page 30.

4 "A Very Unusually Tall [Man]"

p. 16   Reuben Dimond Mussey (1780–1866) was professor of medicine at Dartmouth College.

p. 17   The letter from Reuben Mussey describing Laura is summarized in the introduction to Mary Swift Lamson's book, *Life and Education of Laura Dewey Bridgman, the Deaf, Dumb, and Blind Girl,* pages vi–viii.

p. 18   The Greek War of Independence, which began in 1821, won independence for Greece from the Ottoman Empire. In July 1832, in the Treaty of Constantinople, Greece became a free country, the first of several occupied states to achieve freedom from the Ottomans.

p. 18   Throughout its history, Poland was the pawn of Russia and Prussia (a powerful section of northern Germany), and occasionally Austria. On November 29, 1830, the section of Poland ruled by Russia rose up and fought for its independence. The war lasted until October 5, 1831. Many Europeans and Americans, including Dr. Samuel Gridley Howe, were sympathetic to the Polish struggle.

p. 20 In 1837 when Howe met Julia Brace at the Asylum for the Deaf in Hartford, he figured out a few new approaches to teaching someone Deaf-Blind. Hearing of Laura soon afterward, he was very eager to reach Harmony and Daniel Bridgman and try to persuade them to let him—and not the Hartford Asylum—become their daughter's teacher. Gitter, page 69.

p. 20 Henry Wadsworth Longfellow wrote a letter to his father the evening that Howe met Laura and didn't mention Laura at all. He described only the beautiful scenery of Hanover and his dinner that night with Dr. Reuben Mussey. However, in a later journal entry, Longfellow noted that he had received a letter from Laura written "in her own hand," praising his poem "Evangeline." The letter was found among Longfellow's papers after his death.: Hall and Elliot, page 259.

p. 20 "I shrunk myself . . .": Sanford, page 18.

p. 20 "a large and beautifully-shaped head": This was Howe's first impression of Laura, found on page 27 of Ernest Freeberg's book *The Education of Laura Bridgman: First Deaf and Blind Person to Learn Language.*

p. 21 (caption) "As the most enthusiastic officer . . .": Freeberg, page 66.

p. 21 For information about phrenology, see Freeberg, page 66.

p. 22 "the father of her mind": Elliot and Hall, page 85.

5 Taken Away

p. 23 Various sources cite different dates for Laura's departure for Boston. Lamson says it was October 12; Schwartz says it was October 4. Asa Tenney's reluctance to part with Laura is discussed by Gitter, page 54.

p. 23 "My parents conducted me . . .": Sanford, pages 18–19.

p. 24 "I kept clinging . . .": Sanford, page 19.

p. 25 "Your little girl is in very good health . . .": Elliot and Hall, page 45.

6 What Can Laura Do?

p. 26   "one piece of metal . . .": Elliot and Hall, page 99.

p. 26   The use of electricity as a means of curing ailments is discussed in Lamson, page 88, and in Duffy, page 23.

p. 28   For information on Benjamin Franklin, see John Duffy's *From Humors to Medical Science: A History of American Medicine,* pages 23–24.

p. 29   "Sound comes up . . .": Elliot and Hall, pages 98 and 362.

p. 29   "something in my right foot . . .": Lamson, page 111.

p. 30   "good, hearty laugh": Lamson, page 71.

p. 30   "disagreeable and unladylike": Elisabeth Gitter's article "Deaf-Mutes and Heroines in the Victorian Era," page 188.

p. 30   "refusal to grow . . .": Gitter, "Deaf-Mutes," page 188.

p. 30   "God gave me much voice" appears in Gitter, "Deaf-Mutes," page 188.

p. 30   "doctor" "ship" "pie" "baby": Lamson, page 144.

p. 30   During the time Howe worked with Laura, he also opposed the idea of teaching the deaf to speak. This position may have been a reaction to the masculine sound of her voice. Perhaps he was also influenced by the accepted attitude of the time that women's silence was a virtue. Long after Laura's formal education ended, Howe changed his mind. In 1865 he and Mary Swift Lamson opened a school for the deaf, specializing in speech. Howe decided that by speaking, the deaf would more easily fit into society.

p. 31   For summary of these debates, see Freeberg, *The Education of Laura Bridgman,* pages 31–33, 94–100.

p. 31   "living laboratory": Gitter, "Deaf-Mutes," page 186.

p. 31   "soul jailed to a body": Samuel Gridley Howe's *The Education of Laura Bridgman*, page 9.

7 Words! Words! Words!

p. 33   Louis Braille was born in 1809 in a small town outside of Paris, France. At the age of three, he was blinded from an accident in his father's leather shop. At ten he entered the Royal Institution for Blind Youth in Paris and became a fine cellist and organist, playing church organs all over the country.

Students were taught to read, using a system of raised letters invented by the school's founder. Because these letters were made by pressing paper against copper wire, blind students couldn't use this system to write. And because raised-print books were very expensive to produce, publishers often put two books together in one volume, making them very heavy and cumbersome. A French military man, Charles Barbier, invented a code of twelve raised dots and a number of dashes to allow soldiers to share secret information at night. On a visit to the Royal Institution in 1821, he shared this system. Louis experimented with Barbier's system and, by the age of fifteen, had come up with different arrangements of only six dots, corresponding to letters of the alphabet. Barbier's twelve-dot patterns corresponded to sounds.

Braille's invention allowed the blind person to feel the whole dot pattern for each letter with just the fingertip. The first book in Braille was published in 1827, but the remarkable system was not widely used until 1868, sixteen years after its inventor's death in January 1852. Braille has been adapted to almost all languages, except the Asian ones that use characters rather than letters.

p. 35   "the truth began to flash . . .": Freeberg, page 36. Freeberg also questions whether Laura's breakthrough was as sudden and dramatic as Howe claimed in this passage.

p. 37   (caption) The communication system of hand movements and gestures called sign language evolved at different times in a variety of countries and had no single inventor. American Sign Language, ASL, mostly resembles French sign language. In the 1550s Pedro Ponce de León devised a system of gestures that some authorities call the first formalized sign system. Others cite Juan Pablo Bonet as the first to write a manual containing the finger alphabet, which he did in 1620.

p. 37   "cold as a frog": Elliot and Hall, page 302.

p. 37   "Bread give . . . Water drink . . .": Lamson, page 21.

8 Schoolgirl

p. 40   Daily schedule: Lamson, page 136.

p. 41   How Laura behaved on a typical walk: Freeberg, page 80.

p. 41   "Why does it rain" . . . "Do the words 'think,' 'guess,' . . .": *Child of the Silent Night* by Edith Fischer Hunter, page 111.

p. 42   "Do milliners make stockings?": Lamson, page 141.

p. 43   "Why did God not . . ": Gitter, page 165.

p. 43   "Why are pineapples . . .": Lamson, page 142.

p. 43   "I have four . . . Four senses . . .": Freeberg, "'More Important Than a Rabble of Common Kings,'" page 313.

9 Windows Open

p. 45   "What color is think?": Elliot and Hall, pages 80 and 361.

p. 45   "strongless" . . . "They just aren't.": Lamson, page 110.

p. 45   After Laura's 1839 visit to her parents, she didn't visit her home in Hanover for two more years, and then not again for another four and a half years. Today it's hard to imagine a child having so little contact with her parents. Harmony and Daniel loved their daughter, but they were so busy they sometimes even forgot to write to her.

As recently as thirty-five years ago, most blind children lived in institutions rather than at home, and they visited their parents only during the holidays and for a week or two in the summer. These students didn't enjoy the rough-and-tumble intimacy of family life; indeed, they were somewhat like special guests in their homes. For many of these students, as for Laura, their teachers became their closest friends. Eventually, Samuel Gridley Howe grew worried about the disadvantages of institutional living. In the 1870s he removed the students from dormitories and placed them in small houses, each of which had a matron. He tried to duplicate the home environment.

p. 46   "had a little book . . .": Sanford, page 20.

p. 46   "Will come hundred Sundays": Lamson, page 19.

p. 46   "If you think" . . . "I will have to tell . . .": Freeberg, "'More Important Than a Rabble of Common Kings,'" page 310.

p. 49   "at last the idea . . .": Elliot and Hall, page 71.

10 Weapon or Masterpiece?

p. 50　"pure as Eve": Freeberg, *The Education of Laura Bridgman,* page 165. Howe referred to Laura as "pure and spotless as the petals of a rose": Howe, page 100.

p. 51　"wild schemer" appears in Freeberg, "'More Important Than a Rabble of Common Kings,'" page 323.

p. 51　Horace Mann referred to Laura as "invented" by Howe. Laura could be described as being Howe's "creation," much as the fictional Eliza Doolittle was the creation of Professor Henry Higgins in the play *Pygmalion* by George Bernard Shaw (which was made into the musical *My Fair Lady*).

Elisabeth Gitter (page 158) says that Howe thought of Laura as his creation. In some sense, Laura was, because he chose the teachers and techniques for teaching her. His influence on her *was* immeasurable. But Laura had other influences in her life: her female teachers, her family, other students, her own vibrant curiosity, and an independent spirit. She was not a passive pupil but an active learner, always questioning and challenging her teachers. She was no more a puppet or mouthpiece for her teacher than Eliza Doolittle was for hers. Both women, the real and the fictional, became their own persons with their own strong wills.

p. 52　(caption) While at Perkins, Anne Sullivan learned the finger alphabet from an elderly Laura Bridgman. Anne had trouble finding work, so she was happy to receive an offer to teach a Deaf-Blind girl from Alabama. Anne met seven-year-old Helen Keller in March 1887 and worked with her until her own death in 1936.

p. 53　"had the grief of parting . . .": Lamson, page 84.

p. 53　"I was very strongly attached . . .": Gitter, *The Imprisoned Guest,* page 79.

p. 53　"Where were you? . . .": Elliot and Howe, page 181.

p. 53　After Howe married in 1843, Laura wrote to his brother-in-law, who was a Frenchman, in French. Elliot and Hall, page 177.

p. 54　(caption) "my dearest teacher": Gitter, page 200.

p. 55　"Al-two . . .": Lamson, page 21.

11 "Is God Ever Surprised?"

p. 56   "Doctor says I am . . .": Elliot and Hall, page 84.

p. 56   "Few children are so affectionate . . .": Lamson, page 55.

p. 57   "God is angry . . .": Elliot and Hall, page 83.

p. 58   "Why do you not teach me . . .": Lamson, page 307.

p. 58   "think exactly alike . . .": Gitter, page 205.

p. 58   "Is there a door . . ." and "How large . . .": Freeberg, *The Education of Laura Bridgman,* page 153.

p. 58   "Does God know Latin?" and "Is God ever surprised?": Gitter, page 165.

p. 58   "Does God know as much . . .": Freeberg, page 154.

p. 58   "Why do I have two thoughts? . . .": Lamson, page 282.

p. 58   "I will go home" . . . "little slow.": Lamson, page 46.

p. 60   "My left hand harmed me": Elliot and Hall, page 182.

p. 60   Laura was friends with Oliver Caswell. As long as he didn't get the lion's share of attention from their teachers, Laura was not jealous of him. She also tried to be friends with Lucy Reid and Julia Brace, but they didn't stay at Perkins very long. Laura's teachers became her closest friends. Lydia Drew Morton and Mary Swift Lamson invited her often to their homes for vacations. For a time she considered her brother Addison a good friend. She wrote him many letters. But when Addison moved away from Hanover, Laura turned her attention to her sister Mary. She wrote Mary endless letters. But Mary died in 1859 at the age of seventeen, also of scarlet fever.

12 Famous

p. 63   The idea that Charles Dickens likened Laura to his character Little Nell: Gitter, page 123.

p. 63   "Her face . . .": Charles Dickens, *American Notes,* pages 28, 29.

p. 63   (caption) "even an ordinary . . .": Charles Darwin, *The Descent of Man,* page 464.

p. 64   "best-dressed": Lamson, p. 23.

p. 65   (caption) Sophia Peabody was pressured by her sister to make her husband, Nathaniel Hawthorne, write a memoir of Laura. The sister asked if Hawthorne could spare an evening in Boston to meet with Howe and his pupil. But Hawthorne didn't agree to such an interview and, unlike Dickens and Darwin, never wrote about Laura.

p. 67   "Are ladies afraid of me?": Lamson, page 47.

13 Farewells

p. 68   "Does Doctor love me . . . ?": Lamson, page 213.

p. 70   Uncle Asa never learned the manual alphabet. Asa's letters to Laura always contained misspellings, so perhaps he had trouble memorizing the different finger arrangements.

p. 70   "house assistant": Elliot and Hall, page 299.

p. 72   "They consented for me . . .": Gitter, page 270.

p. 72   "best earthly friend. . . .": Lamson, page 358.

p. 72   "I think much of Dr. H. . . .": Lamson, page 358.

p. 73   "dearly beloved and adopted father": Gitter, page 271.

p. 73   "I am so highly honored . . .": Elliot and Hall, pages 320–21.

p. 75   "You have not taught her . . .": Gitter, *The Imprisoned Guest,* page 282.

p. 75   "I have felt poorly . . .": Elliot and Hall, page 325.

p. 75   *Moth*—. . . .": Gitter, page 283.

Afterword: If Laura Were Alive Today

p. 76   According to the Helen Keller National Center for Deaf-Blind Youths and Adults, a person is considered Deaf-Blind if he or she:

1. has a central visual acuity of 20/200 or less in the better eye with the best corrective lenses (i.e., sees at 20 feet what most people see at 200 feet), or has a field of vision of less than 20 degrees (limited peripheral vision, left and right)

2. has a chronic hearing impairment so that most speech cannot be understood with the best amplification

This definition is abridged; for a full version, see the HKNC website.

p. 83   "Obstacles are things . . .": Elliot and Hall, page 333.

Bibliography

Brewer, David. *The Greek War of Independence: The Struggle for Freedom from Ottoman Oppression and the Birth of the Modern Greek Nation.* Woodstock, N.Y.: Overlook Press, 2001.

Clogg, Richard. *A Concise History of Greece.* Cambridge Concise Histories. New York: Cambridge University Press, 1992.

Darwin, Charles. *The Origin of Species* and *The Descent of Man.* New York: Modern Library, 1936.

Davies, Norman. *Heart of Europe: The Past in Poland's Present.* Rev. ed. New York: Oxford University Press, 2001.

Dickens, Charles. *American Notes.* New York: St. Martin's Press, 1985.

Duffy, John. *From Humors to Medical Science: A History of American Medicine.* 2nd ed. Urbana and Chicago: University of Illinois Press, 1993.

Elliot, Maud Howe, and Florence Howe Hall. *Laura Bridgman: Dr. Howe's Famous Pupil and What He Taught Her.* Boston: Little, Brown, 1903.

Finger, Stanley. *Doctor Franklin's Medicine.* Philadelphia: University of Pennsylvania Press, 2006.

Freeberg, Ernest. *The Education of Laura Bridgman: First Deaf and Blind Person to Learn Language.* Cambridge, Mass.: Harvard University Press, 2001.

———. "'More Important Than a Rabble of Common Kings': Dr. Howe's Education of Laura Bridgman." *History of Education Quarterly* 34 (1994): 305–27.

Gitter, Elisabeth. *The Imprisoned Guest: Samuel Howe and Laura Bridgman, the Original Deaf-Blind Girl.* New York: Farrar, Straus and Giroux, 2001.

———. "Deaf-Mutes and Heroines in the Victorian Era." *Victorian Literature and Culture* 20 (1992): 179–96.

———. "Charles Dickens and Samuel Gridley Howe." *Dickens Quarterly* 8 (1991): 162–67.

———. "Laura Bridgman and Little Nell." *Dickens Quarterly* 8 (1991): 75–79.

Howe, Samuel Gridley. *The Education of Laura Bridgman.* Boston: Perkins, 1893.

Hunter, Edith Fisher. *Child of the Silent Night.* Boston: Houghton Mifflin, 1963.

Keller, Helen. *The Story of My Life.* Hodder and Stoughton, 1904.

———. *Midstream: My Later Life.* New York: Doubleday, 1929.

Lamson, Mary Swift. *Life and Education of Laura Dewey Bridgman, the Deaf, Dumb, and Blind Girl.* Boston: Houghton, Mifflin, 1888.

Lash, Joseph P. *Helen and Teacher: The Story of Helen Keller and Anne Sullivan Macy.* Radcliffe Biography Series. New York: Delacorte Press, 1980.

Longfellow, Henry Wadsworth. *The Letters of Henry Wadsworth Longfellow.* Edited by Andrew Hilen. 6 vols. Cambridge, Mass.: The Belknap Press of Harvard University Press, 1966–82.

Lukowski, Jerzy, and Hubert Zawadzki. *A Concise History of Poland.* 2nd ed. Cambridge Concise Histories. New York: Cambridge University Press, 2006.

Marshall, Megan. *The Peabody Sisters: Three Women Who Ignited American Romanticism.* Boston: Houghton Mifflin, 2005.

Perkins School archives, Watertown, Mass.

Sanford, Edmund C. *The Writings of Laura Bridgman.* San Francisco: Overland Monthly Publishing, 1887.

Schwartz, Harold. *Samuel Gridley Howe, Social Reformer, 1801–1876.* Harvard Historical Studies 67. Cambridge, Mass.: Harvard University Press, 1956.

Websites

Berke, Jamie. "Laura Bridgman and Julia Brace: Predecessors of Helen Keller."
    http://deafness.about.com/cs/deafblind/a/laurajulia.htm
Hearing Health.
    http://www.drf.org/hearing_health/
Perkins School for the Blind.
    http://www.perkins.org
Ruark, Jennifer E. "Unearthing 'the Original Helen Keller.'" *Chronicle of Higher Education*.
    http://www.connsensebulletin.com/keller.html
The Helen Keller National Center for Deaf-Blind Youths.
    http://www.hknc.org
The Laura Dewey Bridgman Collection at the Leonard H. Axe Library, Pittsburg State University, Pittsburg, Kansas.
    http://library.pittstate.edu/spcoll/ndxbridgman.html

Index

Note: Page numbers in **bold** type refer to illustrations.

Adam and Eve, 50
Alexander, Sally, 76, **77,** 78
Americans with Disabilities Act (1990), 78
American Sign Language (ASL), **37,** 89n
Anagnos, Michael, 73
arithmetic, Laura's studies in, 46–48, **47**

Barbier, Charles, 89n
Barrett, James, 16
"Battle Hymn of the Republic" (Howe), 73
Bell, Alexander Graham, 37
Berlin School for the Blind, 18
Bible, 50, 57–58, **59,** 60
Blackie (cat), 14
bleeding:
    with leeches, 2
    as treatment for disease, 1, 2
blistering, as treatment for disease, 1
Bonet, Juan Pablo, 20, 89n
Boston Phrenology Society, 21
Brace, Julia, 20, 38–39
Braille, Louis, 33
Braille Scrabble, 82, **83**
Braille screen communicator, 81, **82**
Braille system, 33, **33,** 78, 81–82, 89n
Bridgman, Addison (brother):
    birth of, 5
    childhood of, 5, 6, 23, 55
Bridgman, Collina (older sister), 3, 4, 10
Bridgman, Collina (younger sister), 55, 75
Bridgman, Daniel (father):
    and Laura's childhood, 6, 16

Bridgman, Daniel (*cont.*)
    and Laura's health problems, 1
    and Laura's home visit, 45
Bridgman, Ellen "Nellie" (sister), 55, 75
Bridgman, Harmony (mother):
    children of, 1, 4, 5, 10, 55
    housework done by, 8–9
    and Laura's childhood, 6
    visits with Laura, 45
Bridgman, John (brother):
    birth of, 5
    childhood of, 5, 6, 23
Bridgman, Laura, **x, 34, 39, 54, 71, 72, 84**
    autobiography of, 85n
    autograph of, 64, **64**
    birth of, 1
    childhood of, 5, 6–11, 52
    communication actions of, 13, 32
    death of, 75
    as education model, 50, 51–52, 67, 80
    electric shocks given to, 26, 28
    failures of communication, 13–15
    fame of, 61, 63–64, 67
    "fits" of, 1, 85n
    handiwork of, 8, **9, 10,** 53, 82
    and Howe, *see* Howe, Samuel Gridley
    illness of, 3–5, 17, 30, 85n
    inheritance of, 72, 82
    intellectual ability of, 25, 31, 36, 39, 60
    isolation of, 10, 52–53, 55
    learning arithmetic, 46–48, **47**
    learning to read, 46

Bridgman, Laura (*cont.*)
    learning to write, 48–49, **48, 49**
    learning words, 32–37, 44–45
    leaving home, 23–25
    loss of senses, 4
    needle used by, 8, **8**
    noises made by, 30
    pain felt by, 30
    personal qualities of, 5, 56–58, 67
    physical examinations of, 28–30
    public appearances of, 61–64, 67, 73
    questions asked by, 36, 41–43, 45, 57–58
    and religion, 56–58, 60
    as role model, 61, 63, 67
    school schedule of, 40–41
    sculpture of, 63–64, **65**
    sense of smell, 4, 29
    sense of sound, 4, 29
    sense of taste, 4, 29
    sense of touch, 6–11, 22, 25, 29
    sight of, 4, 28–29
    speech ability of, 30
    teaching others, **39**, 46, 52, 74, 82
    tombstone of, **77**
    and toys, 11
    vibrations sensed by, 29, 44, 67
Bridgman, Mary (older sister), 3, 4, 10
Bridgman, Mary (younger sister), 55, 92n
Bridgman, Milo (brother), 85n

calisthenics (physical exercise), 41
calomel, 3, 4
camphor, 3
Caswell, Oliver, 38–39, **39**, 60
Charles, Ray, 80
children, and original sin, 50
Child's Book, A, in raised letters, 46
cleansing, as treatment for disease, 1
cochlear implants, 78, **79**
communication:
    actions for, 13, 32

communication (*cont.*)
    adjectives, 44–45
    alphabet on metal squares, **35**
    conversation, 36–37, 44
    fingerspelling, **36**, 37, 61, 74
    learning language, 38–39, 63
    learning to read, 33, 46
    learning to write, 48–49, **48, 49**
    learning words, 32–37, 44–45
    modern devices for, 78, **79**, 80
    sign language, **37**, 89n
compresses, hot, 2

daguerreotype, **24**
Dartmouth College, **17**
Darwin, Charles, 63, **63**
Deaf/Blind people:
    attitudes toward, 70, 78, 79–80
    Braille system for, 33
    communicating through actions, 13, 32
    considered hopeless cases, 16
    definition of, 93n
    education of, 18, 20, 50–52, 78, 80
    fingerspelling, **36**, 37, 61, 74
    illnesses of, 85–86n
    independence of, 80–84
    institutional vs. home living for, 90n
    job possibilities for, 82–83
    known cases of, 20
    laws about, 78
    learning arithmetic, 46–48, **47**
    learning language, 38–39
    learning to write, 48–49, **48**
    medical practices for, 78, **79**
    sign language of, **37**, 89n
    teaching words to, 32–37
    technology in aid of, 80–83
    today, 76–84
    "touch reading" system for, 33
Dickens, Charles, 15, **15**, 63

disease:
    meningitis, 85n
    modern treatments for, 78
    nineteenth-century treatments for, 1–3,
      26, 28
    rubella, 86n
    scarlet fever, 3–5, 17, 78
    Usher's syndrome, 86n
Dix, Dorothea, 63, 70, **70**
doctors, nineteenth-century, 1–3, 26, 28
Drew, Lydia:
    later visits with, 53, 92n
    as Laura's teacher, 32–37, 41–43, 44, 50,
      52
    marriage of, 53
    and visits to Laura's family, 45–46,
      52–53

education:
    Laura as model for, 50, 51–52, 67, 80
    learning for love of it, 50–52
    teacher training, 51
    theories of, 50
    through fear, 50
electric fish, 26
electricity, Franklin's experiments with, 28
electrotherapy, 26, 28
Erlen, Jonathan, 85

faculties (abilities), 31
fingerspelling, 36, **36,** 37, **37,** 61, 74
Fisher, John, 18
Franklin, Benjamin, 28, **28**
Freeberg, Ernest, 21

Garden of Eden, 50
Greece, war for independence, 18
guide dogs, **77,** 81

Hall, G. Stanley, 30
Hawthorne, Nathaniel, 63, 65

horse-drawn carriage, **24**
Howe, Jeannette, 22, 24, 25, 68
Howe, Julia Romana, 68, 73
Howe, Julia Ward, 68, 70, 73, **73**
Howe, Samuel Gridley, **19, 34, 69**
    death of, 70, 72
    education theories of, 31, 32, 50, 51–52,
      55, 80
    fundraising by, 61
    Laura as "creation" of, 22, 30–31, 57, 67,
      72–73, 91n
    letter to Laura's parents, 25
    marriage of, 68
    meeting of Laura and, 20, 22
    motto of, 84
    other interests of, 18, 70
    phrenology as interest of, 20, 21
    and religion, 56–58, 60
    and school for blind children, 18–20, 22,
      27
    teaching words to Laura, 32–37, **34**
humors, 1, **2**

ipecac, 3
Irwin, Bill, 79

Keller, Helen, 40, 63
    childhood of, 74–75, **74**
    and Sullivan as teacher, 52, **66,** 67,
      74–75
    understanding language, 38, 66
Keller, Kate Adams, 63

Lamson, Mary Swift, *see* Swift, Mary
language, age for learning, 38–39
leeches, 2
Locke, John, **31**
Longfellow, Henry Wadsworth, 20

Macy, Anne Sullivan, *see* Sullivan, Anne
Mann, Horace, 50, **51**

manual alphabet, **36,** 37
Matlin, Marlee, 80
medical practices, current, 78, **79**
medicines, in nineteenth century, 1, **2,** 3
meningitis, 85n
mental retardation, 57
Mussey, Reuben Dimond, 16–17

Nero, Emperor, 26
New England:
    farmhouse work in, 8, 10
    typical farmhouse of, **7**
New England Institution for the Education
        of the Blind, 18–20, 22, **27**
    Laura's arrival at, 24–25
    see also Perkins Institution

opium, 3
original sin, 50, 57

Peabody, Sophia, 63, 65, 92–93n
Perkins, Thomas H., 19
Perkins Institution/Perkins School for the
        Blind, 27, **42,** 70, 73
    classroom at, **40**
    daily schedule at, 40–41
    globe at, 61, **62**
    as Laura's home, 70, 73–74
    students on exhibit at, 61
    Sullivan as student at, 52
phrenology, 20, **21**
physical exercise, 41
Poland, war for independence, 18
Ponce de León, Pedro, 89n
poultices, 5

Reed, Lucy, 38–39
religion:
    and the Bible, 50, 57–58, **59,** 60
    good and evil, 50, 57, 60
    Laura learning about, 56–58, 60

religion (*cont.*)
    and morality, 56
    and original sin, 50, 57
    Unitarianism, 57
Rogers, Eliza, 53, 57
rubella (German measles), 86n
Ruggles, Stephen Preston, 62

scarlet fever, 3–5, 17, 78
Scarlet Letter, The (Hawthorne), **33,** 65
screen Braille communicator, 81, **82**
sign language, **37,** 89n
Smithdas, Robert, 80
South Boston (map), **25**
Stoffel, Scott, 80
Sullivan, Anne (Macy), 51–52, **52**
    Keller as pupil of, 52, **66,** 67, 74–75
    learning to fingerspell, 52, 82
Sullivan, Tom, 79
sweating, as treatment for disease, 1–2
Swift, Mary:
    later visits with, 92n
    as Laura's teacher, 53, 54, 55, 57–58
    marriage of, 68
    and school for the deaf, 88n

tabula rasa, 31
tactual fingerspelling, 36
Tenney, Asa, 12–13, 14, 23, 46, 70

Unitarianism, 57
Ursula (guide dog), **77**
Usher's syndrome, 86n

Weihenmayer, Erik, 79
Wight, Sarah, **54,** 55, 58, 68
Wonder, Stevie, 80